The Black Dilemma
by John Herbers

Conflict and Compromise:
The Dynamics of American Foreign Policy
by Richard Halloran

Eastern Europe in the Soviet Shadow
by Harry Schwartz

Madman in a Lifeboat:
Issues of the Environmental Crisis
by Gladwin Hill

The USSR Today
by Harry A. Rositzke

The New York Times
SURVEY SERIES

THEODORE M. BERNSTEIN
GENERAL EDITOR

The New York Times SURVEY SERIES comprises books that deal comprehensively yet comprehensibly with subjects of wide interest, presenting the facts impartially and drawing conclusions honestly.

The series draws on the great information resources of *The New York Times* and on the talents, backgrounds and insights of specially qualified authors, mostly members of the *Times* staff.

The subjects range from the relatively particular problems of civilized life to the broadest conceivable problems concerning whether civilized life, or any kind of life, will continue to be possible on this planet.

The hope is that the books will be essentially informative, perhaps argumentative, but beyond that stimulative to useful, constructive thinking by the citizens who ultimately must share in civilization's decisions.

Madman in a Lifeboat

Madman in a Lifeboat

ISSUES OF THE ENVIRONMENTAL CRISIS

GLADWIN HILL

The John Day Company
An Intext Publisher
NEW YORK

Copyright © 1973 by The New York Times Company

All rights reserved. No part of this book may be reprinted, or reproduced or utilized in any form or by any electronic, mechanical or other means, now known or hereafter invented, including photocopying and recording, or in any information storage and retrieval system, without permission in writing from the Publisher.

Published in hardcover by
The John Day Company, 257 Park Avenue South, New York, N.Y. 10010

Published in softcover by
Intext Press, 257 Park Avenue South, New York, N.Y. 10010

Published on the same day in Canada by Longman Canada Limited.

Printed in the United States of America

Library of Congress Cataloging in Publication Data

Hill, Gladwin.
    Madman in a lifeboat.

    (New York times survey series)
    1. Environmental policy—United States. 2. Human ecology. I. Title.
HC110.E5H54   301.31'0973   72-2436
ISBN: 0-381-98120-7 (hardcover)
         0-381-90000-2 (paperback)

Contents

	Preface	ix
1	Madman in a Lifeboat	3
2	"When Will It Go Away?"	7
3	Population: When Do We Start Stopping?	13
4	Resources: The Sanctimonious Exploiters	21
5	Land: 60,000 Fast-Buck Operators	30
6	Air Pollution: Half the Cards Are Wild	41
7	Water Pollution: The Land of Open Sewers	48
8	Solid Waste: In the Footsteps of the Cave Man	56
9	The Big Myth: "We Can't *Afford* to Be Clean..."	63
10	The States: How to Stack a Pollution Board	70
11	Industry: "Trust Everybody—But Cut the Cards..."	79

12	Government: Rebuilding the One-Hoss Shay	86
13	International Action: The Coming Showdown	94
14	Citizen Action: The Key to Tomorrow	103
	Some Sources	113
	Index	115

Preface

Environmental problems are innumerable, and so, it seems, are books about them.

Therefore it seems incumbent on a writer to give some explanation of why he has the temerity to add yet another volume to the procession.

The purpose of this book is *not* to engage, once again, in a tedious descriptive inventory of environmental problems, with which most people by now are all too familiar. Readers won't find here any repetitive rundowns on the Alaska pipeline, preservation of the whale, or the "death" of Lake Erie, although all of these are worthy subjects.

The purpose of this book is to spotlight major *issues* on which reform in the principal environmental problem areas hinges; to shatter some widespread myths and fallacies; to delineate some avenues of reform; and above all to call attention to our idiotic failure to develop national policies on many of these problems.

GLADWIN HILL

December, 1972

Madman in a Lifeboat

1

Madman in a Lifeboat

> At the beginning of 1970, there was as yet no national legislative, administrative or judicial policy on environmental problems. Jack C. Oppenheimer and Leonard A. Miller, Washington lawyers, in the Annals of the American Academy of Political and Social Science, May 1970.

IF A WEALTHY MAN told you he would give you an incomparably pleasant island, stocked with a certain quantity of supplies and amenities, to be occupied by you and as many friends as you cared to invite, providing you would live there permanently, and if you were intrigued by the proposition, there are some obvious facts any reasonably bright person would ascertain at the outset.

You would want to know how big the island was; how many people it would comfortably accommodate; and how long, with a given number of inhabitants, the supplies and amenities would hold out. On the basis of these facts you would decide how many friends it would be feasible to take with you; what scale of living you could look forward to, given the limited quantity of supplies; and how your activi-

MADMAN IN A LIFEBOAT

ties might be structured to prolong this idyllic existence as long as possible.

The human race is essentially in the position of people who have embarked on such an island venture. Mankind has undertaken to live on the surface of a spherical spacecraft of very limited size (only 8,000 miles in diameter), with a limited store of supplies—and hopes to do it indefinitely.

Yet the last thing mankind has given much consideration to is making an inventory of its living space and resources, adjusting the number of users accordingly, and balancing the two in a way that will be viable through what we call eternity.

Instead, what actually has happened, over the million-plus years that man has inhabited the earth, is more like a familiar vignette from the movies. Most people have seen Hollywood's standard depiction of stranded men in a lifeboat. The first thing they do, not knowing how long it may be before they are rescued, is to take stock of their emergency rations and apportion them to last as long as possible.

But there's always one man in the lifeboat who, after a time, gets a glazed look in his eyes and starts voraciously cramming down his throat all the food and water he can grab. That connotes, in the Hollywood idiom, that he has gone mad. He is usually conked with an oar and regretfully dropped to the sharks.

Up to now, over these million years, mankind has behaved pretty much like the madman in the lifeboat.

Except for scholars doodling abstractly, no one has really assessed how much usable room there is on man's small spacecraft; analyzed the resources in the skin-thin working layer on the surface of the earth; or thought about a suitable apportionment of space and resources for the eternity to which most people pay lip service. Instead, man has prolifer-

Madman in a Lifeboat

ated indiscriminately, ignored the exigencies of living space, consumed resources as if there were no tomorrow and, to boot, has littered the land, sea, and skies with the wastes of his consumption until they threaten to smother and poison him.

There is no one around to clout mankind on the head with an oar and bring a halt to this madness, but nature has mercifully started to do it. Suddenly, in the last few of these million years, the overburdened land, sea, and skies have begun hurling back in man's face the residues of his profligacy.

The symptoms of mankind's irrationality are visible in various degrees all over the world. But nowhere are they better—or worse—epitomized than in the United States.

We are the most affluent nation in the world and supposedly the most "advanced," whatever that means. We look down on the amoeba-like reproduction in nations like India and China. Yet we have never given any systematic thought to what the optimum population of our own country might be. We not only have no collective restraints on reproduction but seemingly we are afraid, as a nation, even to ask the question.

Seventy-five per cent of our population is crammed into less than 3 per cent of our land area, engendering insupportable urban problems. Yet we have never, in two hundred years, considered how the rest of the land might best be used. We constitute only 6 per cent of the world's population, yet month in and month out we consume something like half the resources flowing in the world's commerce.

We haven't, collectively, ever asked ourselves how long this can go on before other nations take steps to stop this greediness. Indeed, they may be doing that already. It seems more than possible that many of the international frictions, dislocations, and pressures that bedevil us daily are expressions, however subconscious, of resentment and rebellion against our greed.

And, finally, having "led the world" in everything else—except serenity—we have set new records in despoiling our environment with wastes and ill-considered treatment of our natural heritage.

What lies ahead?

Both nationally and globally the outlook has grim and bright aspects.

On the one hand are the sorry results of centuries of human recklessness. On the other hand is the consideration that, for 99 per cent of that time, we were quite oblivious of our malfeasance. That attitude has suddenly changed. Not only in the United States but throughout most of the world, there is growing awareness of the environmental crunch.

Unfortunately, both internationally and in the United States, we're still at the stage where there's more talk than action about problems that call for action urgently. Until we come to grips with these difficulties and solve them, we will continue to be just like the madman in a lifeboat.

2

"When Will It Go Away?"

ALMOST DAILY someone comes up to me, refers in some way to what is now widely called the environmental crisis, and asks plaintively, "When is it going to go away?"

My standard answer is that it isn't going to go away—that it's like venereal disease: it will just keep on getting worse until decisive steps are taken to cure it. This applies not only to the obvious things like air pollution, water pollution, and the solid waste bugbear but also to less obvious but more fundamental problems: population, consumption of natural resources, land use.

Happily, the stubbornness of these woes is being countered at this moment by a force that promises to be equally persistent.

I call it the Environmental Revolution.

Revolution doesn't necessarily mean violence and bloodshed. Its essential elements are (1) radically changed standards, and (2) shifts in the placement of power

Both these features are conspicuous in the environmental ferment that is now going on.

The standards undergoing radical change are those applying to the "quality of life."

We have suddenly awakened to the fact that after more than a million years of human travail, most of us do not live as well as the cave man lived. He at least had assurance of pure water, clean air, uncontaminated food, and unsullied views. Very few people in the United States have these assurances today.

The awareness that, with all our material progress, all our sophistication, we aren't as well off in some basic respects as the cave man has crystallized a tremendous mass demand that we retrieve these natural blessings.

Sir Isaac Newton said that every action has an equal and opposite reaction. What we are seeing right now is a long-delayed reaction to the Industrial Revolution which began changing the civilized world in the eighteenth century.

This is the counterrevolution. People want the benefits of industrialization and technology. But they've suddenly decided that the price isn't right: that we're paying too much in terms of a degraded environment. And when a large number of people decide that the price of something isn't right, that thing is doomed.

Public discontent reached a crescendo in the Earth Day observances of April 22, 1970. Upward of twenty million people are estimated to have taken some active part in that event, and there could not have been many people in the country who did not at least hear about it.

"But can this interest be sustained?" was the question asked innumerable times in the wake of Earth Day.

The answer obviously was no—not sustained at the holiday pitch that even impelled Congress to recess so that its members could participate.

"When Will It Go Away?"

But neither could everyone go back to business as usual. The dilemmas remained. Public concern about doing something about them had been aroused—irrevocably. The ensuing months have borne this out. You can't pick up anything (to paraphrase the naturalist John Muir) in which somebody doesn't use the word "environment." The word "ecology," not long ago utterly arcane to most people, is part of the official title of a government department in the State of Washington.

The President's Council on Environmental Quality is a going concern, and no federal agency is supposed to mount a project without circulating a prospectus on its "environmental impact." In the biggest cabinet-level reshuffle in many years, a score of federal agencies have been yanked from their historic moorings and clustered in the independent Environmental Protection Agency.

The manifestations of continued public concern are endless. Citizens have taken up the cudgels against phosphates in detergents and against nonreturnable bottles. And there is a rising chorus of public insistence on taking part in the "decision-making process" on environmental questions.

What brought about the degradation of our environment?

Superficially it's just a gigantic case of sloppy national housekeeping on the part of communities, on the part of industry, and on the part of government, but there's something much more fundamental behind it.

Environmental degradation came about because of a breakdown in the democratic process. Trace back any of our environmental problems and you end up at the same place: they are all conditions that are now so pervasive that the real remedy lies in governmental action. By the same token, these conditions could have been *averted* by governmental action. Why weren't they?

Demonstrably because in each instance the public, or some segment of it, failed to think about where we were heading environmentally and failed to express itself on where we should be heading.

An example is the River and Harbor Act of 1899. One section of it provided that no fluids except municipal sewage could be discharged into waterways without a permit from the Army Corps of Engineers. Although there were occasional minor prosecutions for discharging *without* permits, the permit feature of the law was not implemented for seventy years. (The only permits issued under the law in that time related to the obstruction of navigation, not pollution.)

Why wasn't the law enforced? Manifestly because there was no great public outcry for it to be implemented. The public, in effect, had abdicated its role in the decision-making process.

Why?

I think it is because we became a nation of spectators, of people who subconsciously assumed that effective administration of national and even local affairs is something that you buy, prepackaged, like frozen spinach at the market . . . for the price of taxes and a vote cast every four years for President, every two years for congressmen and state legislators.

That assumption, of course, was a mistake. And the most dramatic evidence of the fact has been the tobogganing pace of environmental deterioration.

Belatedly, and perhaps in many cases subconsciously, people have become aware of this abdication. They are scrambling to regain the reins of power, clamoring for a revival of

"When Will It Go Away?"

their role in the decision-making process. This scramble is the Environmental Revolution.

Shifts in power are always unpleasant for somebody. These stresses are being experienced now by all segments of our society, and are the reason for much of the lamentation and bewilderment surrounding environmental problems. A shift in power means that somebody has to relinquish some degree of authority or autonomy. We see this happening on every side.

In the cause of environmental reform, citizens are being told that they cannot have backyard incinerators. They are being told how their cars shall be equipped.

The federal government, in efforts to abate pollution, has moved into jurisdictional areas the states once considered sacrosanct. States are abridging erstwhile autonomies of cities. The states and the federal government are making certain decisions regarding processes and waste discharges that industry once considered its sole prerogative. And to round out the circle, citizens are newly asserting themselves in areas long left to bureaucratic decision—such as the routing of highways, the establishment of air and water quality standards, and the location and responsibilities of industry.

Other subtle shifts in power are taking place outside conventional channels. The problem of sewage facilities is being used as a device to regulate influxes of population. Labor, through such tactics as trash-removal strikes, is using pollution as a bargaining weapon. Conversely, environmental policies are cropping up as issues in labor negotiations. In the 1970 national elections a number of congressmen and at least one governor were defeated by margins indisputably attributable to the "conservation vote." And the indications are that in future elections this influence will continue to grow.

There is no way of keeping score on these shifts of power. Bits of sovereignty cannot be counted like poker chips. The point is that a sweeping realignment of influence is in progress. And it is due essentially to the reassertion of public opinion through many channels, in decisions directed at environmental reform.

If this renaissance of public awareness reaches the proportions indicated, it will yield a double dividend. We will end up with an improved "quality of life." And the democratic process will achieve new meaning.

3
Population: When Do We Start Stopping?

WE LAUGH TODAY at the fact that people once refused to believe that the earth was round.

Yet we are guilty of a worse asininity.

People refuse to believe that the earth is finite, that there is a fixed limit on its size, and that it is never going to get any bigger. This sphere has an immutable surface area of 196,940,000 square miles. Most of this is ocean. The land area is less than sixty million square miles.

With approximately 3.5 billion people on the globe today, that gives a theoretical population density of approximately sixty persons per square mile. Actually the density is much greater, because two-thirds of that land area is unsuitable for settlement under our present technology and mores. These space limitations are reflected in the fact that in 1850 there were only four cities in the world with more than a million population. By 1900 there were fifteen such cities. By 1960 the number had jumped to 141.

The world's population increases by 7,900 people every hour. At this rate, thirty-five years from now there will be seven billion people, instead of the present 3.5 billion.

If this does not seem important, consider what this growth rate implies. It means that, almost within the lifetime of people now living, there could be *ten* people on earth for every one there is now. Even people disposed to be complacent should be able to visualize how intolerable that would be. Today somewhere between one-third and one-half of all the people in the world do not have enough to eat. Upward of 10,000 people die of starvation every week.

Enlargement of the effective world food supply is running far behind the growth of population. Some scientists, such as Dr. Paul Ehrlich, biologist at Stanford University, foresee massive famines as early as the mid-1970's. Apart from food, the growth of many a nation's economic base is running far behind the population increase.

In most of the underdeveloped countries—which contain around 70 per cent of the world's population—population at the present rate of increase will double in twenty years or less. That means that to maintain even the present low standard of living there would also have to be a doubling in twenty years of all the facilities that make up that standard of living: housing, transportation, hospitals, schools, power plants, and industrial production. The prospect of such a broadening of economic bases is virtually nil.

Assistant Secretary of the Interior Stanley Cain observed in 1967, regarding international assistance programs: "After two decades of postwar technical assistance, the statistics show a worsened, not improved, condition for the vast majority of the two billion people of the poor countries.

"The billions of dollars, and of pounds and rubles, have not bettered the great masses of individuals in Asia, Africa, and Latin America. In general, food on a per capita basis is

Population: When Do We Start Stopping?

less than it was before World War II, and the amenities and the human rights are static or worsened."

In March 1969 the U.S. Agency for International Development reported to Congress that potential benefits from $9 billion in aid to Latin American countries in seven years had been "largely canceled out" in terms of per capita improvement because of "staggeringly high" birth rates. The agency noted drily that the question of population control had been excluded from aid policies because of its "political volatility." In outlining a program of "fundamental and sweeping reforms" in foreign aid in September 1970, President Richard Nixon said nothing about the population-limitation problem.

In his book *Population/Resources/Environment*, Dr. Ehrlich cites a small sample of what the population-resource imbalance implies. El Salvador had a population density of 782 persons per square mile of arable land. In adjacent Honduras, the density was only 155 persons. Nearly 300,000 El Salvadorians moved into Honduras in search of land and employment. The resulting frictions caused a war in 1969, quelled only by the intervention of the Organization of American States.

A great deal of sophistry has been resorted to in efforts to talk away the population problem rather than solve it. Much of the nonsense has centered on food. Statistics about increased grain production here and there are cited as evidence that the world easily can feed more millions. Such statistics blithely ignore the fact that grain is not equivalent to nutrition, that grain is such an *uncritical* food item (lacking in proteins and fats) that some groups, such as Eskimos, get along without it entirely.

Even statistics on food production in general are deceptive. Production is not the same thing as getting food into people's stomachs. Dr. Ehrlich calculated it would take a train 3,000 miles long to contain grain that is grown every year in India, but which is eaten by rats. Even when food gets to market, millions of people simply don't have the money to buy it.

It used to be a scientific cliché that the oceans were a vast potential larder of food for the world. More recent realistic studies have shown that, except for unusable microscopic life, great expanses of the ocean are biological deserts.

Great store also has been put in the Green Revolution—the use of new high-yield seeds, chemicals, and advanced farming methods—as the prospective solution of the food problem. Perhaps the most authoritative commentary on that came from Dr. Norman Borlaug, a specialist in high-yield corn and wheat, who received the Nobel Peace Prize in 1970 as a leading warrior in the Green Revolution. He said, "Unless we strike a proper balance between population and food resources, we will face more and more problems and the Green Revolution will have been useless."

All the evidence points to the fact that the global "population explosion" must be stopped by whatever action necessary, and that this cannot be started soon enough. The doubling of the world's population in the next thirty-five years is already inevitable, implicit in the reproductive patterns of people already here. But every day that passes without action makes the future problems worse.

In the face of these grim facts, the reaction of most world governments, particularly the United States, has been retrogressive rather than enlightened. In 1967 the United Nations produced a declaration subscribed to by some thirty nations that said:

Population: When Do We Start Stopping?

"The Universal Declaration of Human Rights describes the family as the natural and fundamental unit of society. It follows that any choice and decision with regard to the size of the family must irrevocably rest with the family itself, and cannot be made by anyone else."

(Granting that the family is the fundamental unit of society, why "it follows" that any family has any right to proliferate—or do anything else—without regard to public safety and the general welfare is hard to see.)

Similarly, President Nixon, in 1969, while sending a widely praised message to Congress recommending consideration of population problems, virtually negated any substance in it by forswearing any decisive governmental action to limit population. Referring to "stabilization" (i.e., limitation) of population, he said, "Clearly, in no circumstances will the activities associated with the pursuit of this goal be allowed to infringe on the religious convictions or personal wishes and freedom of any individual, nor will they be allowed to impair the absolute right of all individuals to have such matters of conscience respected by public authorities."

This view received no support from a committee of the National Academy of Sciences, which concurrently reported, in an exhaustive study, titled "Resources and Man": "Population control is the absolute primary essential without which all other efforts are nullified. Our Department of Health, Education and Welfare should adopt the goal of real population *control* both in North America and throughout the world.

"Ultimately this implies that the community and society as a whole, and not only parents, must have a say about the number of children a couple may have."

(President Nixon's "absolute right" of people to beget as many children as their glands, whims, and carelessness impel them to is, of course, a right that is documented nowhere. The right of society to limit population is palpably as valid and inescapable as its acknowledged right to limit in the name of public safety the number of people who are allowed to crowd into a restaurant, theater, or auditorium.)

There are several avenues to population limitation, among them voluntary contraception, sterilization, and abortion. There are also quasi-compulsory methods. These range from governmental economic sanctions against excess child-bearing to a "birth permit" system. The latter would involve wholesale sterilization of the population by such means as chemicals placed in water or food, with temporary antidotes for the sterility issued on a rationed basis.

Such compulsory measures are grim to contemplate. But they are inevitable if voluntary efforts, on a massive global basis, are no more successful than they have been to date. And they are far more civilized than the methods humanity historically has tacitly relied on to reduce population: war, famine, and disease.

But despite such grim prospects, the world's only answer so far has been a plethora of study commissions and tokenism rather than any effective action.

The scope of action that is in order is suggested by a United Nations report in December 1970. It said that to extend "family planning" services to all couples of child-bearing age in only twenty of the underdeveloped countries, applying present contraceptive technology, would require more than 50,000 doctors, 200,000 associated medical personnel, and 350,000 field workers.

Among the many foolish responses to the impending global population crisis, perhaps the most mistaken is the insist-

Population: When Do We Start Stopping?

ence by some pseudo-experts that the United States does not have to think about population limitation because *it* does not have any population problem and *it* has plenty of room. These assumptions at best are questionable, and even if true they are irrelevant.

Despite the seeming abundance of space, there are some responsible scientists who think that the United States has long since passed its optimum population level. One indication is the worsening unmanageability of the big cities that harbor the mass of our population. These "megalopolitan" concentrations could be dispersed and before too long almost certainly will have to be. However the population is distributed, the fact remains that as you increase the number of people, their web of interrelationships starts to become unbearably complicated.

A well-known sociological phenomenon is this: two individuals have only a dual relationship, A to B and B to A. Add one more person and you have a *six-way* pattern: A to B, B to C, C to A, and the reverse. The complexity and interdependence increase at a staggering geometrical rate. This interdependence involves everything from employment and food to telephone calls. The increasing complication actually taking place is reflected in the growing number of ways that normal life over large segments of the country can and is being disrupted—by power blackouts, transportation strikes, miscellaneous labor stoppages, epidemics, and economic concatenations. At one time a blood transfusion was a simple person-to-person relationship, with no problems. Today blood supplies have undergone the same depreciation as other mass-production commodities: if you receive blood from a commercial blood bank—a major medical source—

the chance is one in ten that you will get hepatitis, which can be fatal.

But assume the United States is *not* overpopulated now. At the present growth rate, the population will double in about sixty years. There is no difference in principle between the United States' situation and the underdeveloped countries' predicament: it is merely a matter of time. Therefore a confrontation with the problem is vital. And, like pollution, the problem will become harder to deal with the longer it is kept under a rug of study commissions (which can only arrive at facts that are widely known and undisputed) and minuscule appropriations for "family planning."

But the hidden premise that the United States' population situation, whatever it is, can be considered apart from that of the rest of the world is an absurd resort to long-discredited isolationism. If Mexico's population doubles in twenty years, for instance, the differential in living standards will suck millions of people across the border, which physically is almost impossible to seal. There will be Mexicans camping out in backyards in Kansas City. Mexicans are nice people, and this would not be horrendous *per se.* But that's no way to run international affairs.

Exclude from consideration, if you will, even the possibility of a Latin American invasion. There remains the inescapable fact that if there is to be meaningful action taken on the already critical global population problem, the United States must be a prime mover because of its position in the world. And it will make an ineffectual and disastrous appearance in the role if it has itself failed to come to grips with the problem and is still pretending, like the madman in the lifeboat, that there is no tomorrow.

4

Resources: The Sanctimonious Exploiters

THE SANTA BARBARA, California, oil well blowout in January 1969 was the Hiroshima bomb of the Environmental Revolution.

A month earlier, *Fortune* put out an issue devoted entirely to the concerns of youth. It did not mention environment. Less than a year later, the march of events impelled *Fortune* to devote an entire issue to environment.

The national and international impact of the Santa Barbara accident transcended on a cosmic scale the fact that a few million gallons of oil were smeared over a few miles of lovely beaches. The event, dramatizing how nature can strike back when abused, triggered the release of a vast reservoir of public uneasiness about environmental deterioration. Reform was an idea whose time had come.

Implicit in the Santa Barbara imbroglio were the questions: Why were we drilling for oil in the Santa Barbara Channel anyway? Were we so desperate for oil that a celebrated scenic area had to be jeopardized? Was similar abuse in store for other attractive parts of the country? The Santa Barbara riddle epitomized a thousand other environmental anomalies across the nation with which people were familiar. Why were we talking about building a great oil pipeline across Alaska that might do inestimable natural damage? Why were we gouging up national forests and other preserves with mining operations? Why were we turning Lake Erie into a sewage sump?

What obviously angered millions of people was the glaring fact that there was *no* rational answer to the question of why we were drilling for oil in Santa Barbara. There was no pressing need for that particular oil. Foreign countries were clamoring to sell us oil—at considerably cheaper prices than the going rates for oil in the United States. Only a small amount of this oil was being admitted to the United States, under a "quota" system. The limitation caused a tight market in oil, which was the oil industry's justification for drilling for oil wherever it might be found in the United States: in the Gulf of Mexico, in Alaska, in Santa Barbara. . . .

The basic reason oil was smeared on the Santa Barbara beaches, then, was the quota system. Why did it exist?

The quota system was established, at the insistence of the oil industry, in the 1950's, when a great influx of foreign oil had pushed prices down in America and the oil industry was hurting. That was the simple fact of the matter. But the oil industry—which has managed to develop more influence in Washington than any other industry—had an elaborate rationalization for imposing quotas.

They were, the industry said piously, a matter of "national defense": if we imported too much foreign oil we would

Resources: The Sanctimonious Exploiters

become dependent on foreign sources, which could be cut off in time of war.

The argument had enough of a veneer of plausibility to get by. But, as many experts suggested in the ensuing years, it was essentially fallacious.

If a commodity would be of such critical importance in a national emergency, and if it was currently available from both domestic and foreign sources, the average person's instinct would be to husband the domestic supply and make maximum use of the foreign oil before some turn of events *did* cut it off.

Ah, no, said the oil industry. Domestic exploration must be pursued so we know how much oil we have, and so it will be available in case of an emergency.

The fallacy in this is that whenever an oil deposit is discovered, the industry's standard practice is to deplete it. In only four instances—the fields at Elk Hills and Buena Vista hills in California, Teapot Dome in Wyoming, and an adjunct of the Prudhoe Bay discovery in Alaska—has oil actually been impounded as a national defense reserve.

What the restriction on foreign oil does do—like the purported "conservation" practices in the Texas fields that vary from month to month, depending on the price of oil—is to enable the oil industry to charge prices that, repeated federal studies and congressional testimony have attested, cost consumers in the United States an extra $4 billion or more a year.

Economists have suggested that instead of that hidden tax of $4 billion a year, representing a premium of $1.04 a barrel in the price of oil, national defense could be better served by lifting the import quotas and sealing domestic deposits to be ready for use in an emergency. This course, they have calculated, would cost taxpayers only a few cents a barrel.

In 1970 a presidential commission recommended that the quota system be ended, but oil industry pressures prevailed. Quotas were continued—and along with them the oil industry's ostensibly inescapable need to drill for oil even in the Santa Barbara Channel.

Few of the millions of people who were appalled by the Santa Barbara blowout knew all these background details. But they seemed to sense that there was something fishy about the purported necessity of drilling there. And there was.

The oil industry is unique in having constructed such an ingenious mechanism for making money, in the name of national defense, while actually depleting a valuable resource, but the system is no more irrational than the nation's approach to natural resources generally. It is the approach of the madman in the lifeboat: grab, and never mind about tomorrow.

Daily we consume millions of tons of oil, coal, iron, copper, lead, zinc, aluminum, chromium, and dozens of other substances without a thought about how long the supply of these resources will continue. Somewhere in the back of its mind the public has an impression that there is an endless supply of these commodities—the same delusion it had, until brusquely disabused, about the supply of clean water and clean air.

The real facts of the situation are so contradictory to this notion as to be frightening.

The only major nonrenewable resource in the world of which there is a long-term supply is coal. In respect to nearly every other mineral, the known reserves are uncomfortably

Resources: The Sanctimonious Exploiters

small. According to Dr. Preston Cloud, geologist at the University of California and chairman of the "Resources and Man" study, at present consumption rates the world's chromium will be used up by the year 2500; good quality iron will run out somewhat before that; and molybdenum and manganese, two essential metals in our technology, will be gone by 2200.

For many of the more common substances such as oil, tungsten, copper, lead, zinc, tin, gold, silver, and platinum, the prospective exhaustion points come *before* the year 2000 —less than thirty years hence.

Some observers have consoled themselves with the thought that predicted shortages will be offset by new discoveries, or by gradual movement toward lower and lower grade ores. But this notion begs the question that these resources are finite, and however extensive they are, they will run out some day. We have given no thought, in terms of national or international policy, either to the exigency of resource exhaustion or to a day of reckoning that could come even sooner.

A large part of the world's resources come from the underdeveloped or "emerging" nations, which constitute an ever-growing majority of the world's population. How long is it going to be before they become impatient with this disproportionate division of resources—and take whatever steps are necessary to get their share?

The basic determinant of the flow of resources now is price. The price of a ton of copper represents what it costs to mine it, refine it, and distribute it, with profit margins for the various middlemen along the way.

This sort of free-market price system worked fine in the

days when there were relatively few people on the earth and when all indications were that the earth had a greater hoard of resources than could ever be used up. The system is still suited today to *renewable* resources, such as wood, cloth, or eggs. It is treacherous when applied to nonrenewable resources that we can see running out, in some cases, within our lifetime.

There is an ominous parallel between free-market pricing of exhaustible resources and what has happened to us in respect to clean air and clean water. We considered these inexhaustible resources, too. So industry, among others, appropriated waterways as waste disposal channels and the sky as a receptacle for gaseous refuse.

The price of industry's products continued to be simply cost plus profit. The prices did not reflect a hidden cost component: the clean water and clean air in the public domain that was being used, on either a short-term or long-term basis, to produce the products. Now we are confronted with large-scale expenditures (which ultimately the public as a whole will bear) to rehabilitate these damaged portions of the public domain.

The rehabilitation process is far more expensive than it would have been if this hidden item of overhead had been taken into consideration in the first place. To set up a quite hypothetical example, women might have been more frugal in their use of lipsticks if the price had reflected the fact that they were produced at the cost of water pollution that ruined a fine fishing area. A pound of copper consumed today is a pound of copper that just won't be there twenty, fifty, or a hundred years hence, when it may be needed more. When all the world's copper runs out, people will be put to considerable trouble, expense, and perhaps distress to contrive substi-

Resources: The Sanctimonious Exploiters

tutes. In consuming copper so greedily, we are mortgaging the future.

The Public Land Law Review Commission, established by Congress, produced in June 1970 a 342-page report on its five years of study of what should be done with the one-third of the federally owned United States land. Virtually nothing was said about policy regarding the large amount of nonrenewable resources on that land—oil, coal, gas, metals—except tacitly to endorse continued exploitation of them at, if anything, accelerated rates.

Asked about conservation of these resources, a commission official replied off-handedly, "Oh, that was left to the normal operations of the marketplace." These "normal operations" ignore conservation. The universal yardstick is what will turn the biggest profit quickest, what will yield the most dollars *tomorrow,* with no regard for the future.

Environmentally this policy is highly destructive. On Castle Peak in the White Cloud Mountains of Idaho, in the Challis national forest, a mining company is proposing to dig a huge pit a mile and a half long to extract molybdenum ore. We don't need that molybdenum. There is plenty of it on the market from other sources, and the national defense reserve supply has been far above the specified level. But there is profit to be made in extracting that molybdenum—if necessary by undercutting the prices of other molybdenum suppliers.

The same pattern is duplicated by the score across the country. Lake Superior is being polluted to produce iron ore. From the State of Washington to the Mexican border, landscapes are being gouged to produce copper. Thousands of square miles in eastern states have been desolated by strip (open pit) mining for coal. Nobody knows whether these activities, these sacrifices of the nation's natural heritage, are in any degree warranted because nobody has ever taken a long-range look at the world's supply of exhaustible resources and figured out how they can best be husbanded.

There have been many federal "resource commission" studies. But the narrowness of their outlook was indicated in a comment by Secretary of Commerce Maurice Stans in announcing the latest of such inquiries in 1971. "There unquestionably are more mineral resources in the world," he said confidently, "than can be consumed in the next fifty years."

Isn't that fine? In the fifty-first year, the inescapable implication is, humanity can go cut its throat.

An intelligent look at resources, which would have to be both national and international, might produce a pricing system that reflected the inevitable exhaustion of these resources. And the lack of such a realistic approach is what has been making a farce of our efforts to cope with the growing problem of solid waste. Much of it should be dealt with not by the prevailing methods of burning it or burying it, but by recycling it. In the absence of a realistic value system, there is no rationale for recycling any but a few commodities. It's usually far cheaper to extract new materials from the earth than to reprocess the quite usable materials we already have extracted.

There are larger dimensions to the resource problem than the mere gratification of material desires.

In an article in *Science* (June 5, 1970), economist J. Alan Wagar wrote: "The depletion of soils, water tables, minerals, interesting species and space and amenity values must be curbed if future generations are to have a rich life. To accel-

Resources: The Sanctimonious Exploiters

erate the discovery and exploitation of mineral resources, we now give generous depletion allowances. However, to encourage more efficient use of such resources, we may need to institute resource depletion taxes."

If all the foregoing sounds radical, heretical, and tendentious, reflect on the fact that little or none of it is inconsistent with what was said, with politic understatement and restraint, in the 1970 report of the federal Council on Environmental Quality:

Even taking into account such economic factors as increased prices with decreasing availability, it would appear at present that the quantities of gold, platinum, zinc and lead are not sufficient to meet demands. At the present rate of expansion of about 6 per cent a year, silver, tin and uranium may be in short supply even at higher prices by the turn of the century. By the year 2050, several more minerals may be exhausted if the current rate of consumption continues. . . .

We are gaining an increased sophistication about our consumption of natural resources and a better understanding of the limited availability of natural resources. We must begin to translate these new attitudes into effective long-range policies if we are to achieve the goal of a satisfactory environment.

5

Land: 60,000 Fast-Buck Operators

EVERY ONCE in a while you read of a miser dying in a shabby furnished room in one of our big cities, often of malnutrition, among bankbooks that show assets running into six figures.

It's a psychosis. And the United States shows the same symptoms. It is suffering from urban congestion and resultant problems while most of its most valuable resource, land, stands largely unused. The nation covers 3,615,000 square miles—about eleven acres for every man, woman, and child in the country. Yet upward of 75 per cent of the nation's 200 million citizens, as mentioned earlier, live crowded into less than 3 per cent of this space.

One great megalopolitan strip extends for a thousand miles down the East Coast from Boston to Virginia, and soon it will reach all the way to Florida. Another such strip is developing on the West Coast. It now extends almost continuously from San Francisco to the Mexican border; at the present rate it will soon reach up through Washington and Oregon to the Canadian border.

Land: 60,000 Fast-Buck Operators

There is another great megalopolitan concentration in the middle of the country—the Chicago-Milwaukee-Detroit-Cleveland area.

In much of this urban crush, population densities run several times the 4,000 persons per square mile that urban planners say is the maximum for pleasant city existence. The density in Manhattan, the heart of New York City, is 25,000 people per square mile—25 per cent more than that of teeming Tokyo. The consequences of this inordinate congestion are in the daily headlines: squalor, filth, poverty, crime, tensions, riots, and insoluble financial problems.

There is mounting evidence that beyond a certain point in municipal growth the "economies of size" decline: the amenities, from sanitation and traffic management to welfare and schools, become more expensive than the tax base can support. It would cost an enormous amount just to put Manhattan sidewalks into good repair—and nobody is talking about doing it.

Once there were reasons for this dense congregation of people in metropolises. They originally settled on the coasts, where ships and water power were available. The climate was more equable than in many parts of the country. In the days of manual labor, there was a demand for a large number of workers. As commerce developed there was the need for the daily face-to-face confrontations of the marketplace. The "economies of size" caused cities to reach out and absorb outlying areas, getting bigger and bigger.

None of these reasons is compelling any more. Shipping has become less important. Power can be developed or transmitted anywhere. Personal climate is so controllable that living in a 100-degree desert is as feasible as living in a temperate area. Unskilled manual labor has become almost as rare a livelihood as watchmaking. Modern communications have made daily marketplace confrontations unnecessary. Yet the great urban concentrations persist and worsen, out of inertia. And their problems become more numerous and insoluble.

And, out of inertia, the same three-quarters of the nation's land remains in the limbo of the frontier days. Half the nation's land is still classified, geographically and functionally, as farmland. But only a fraction of it is needed or used for agriculture. About 5 per cent of our population lives on it. Another 25 per cent of the nation's land is forested. Only 8 per cent is urban.

The underlying reason for this paradox is simply that the nation as a whole has never taken an inventory of its land and considered how it could be used most advantageously to accommodate a growing population. The last large-scale consideration of the problem was a century ago, when Congress passed the Homestead Act to encourage settlement of the West. A pioneer could become the owner of land by occupying and developing it. The homesteading process reached its peak, not in the nineteenth century as many suppose, but in the World War I era, when wheat farming became very profitable. Since then a series of restrictions on federal land has virtually ended homesteading, although the law is still on the books.

In the absence of comprehensive consideration of how the nation's land might be used, one-third of it—some 750 million acres—has been left under sketchy and admittedly unsatisfactory federal management. Utilization decisions about the other two-thirds, under the hoary states' rights philosophy, have been fragmented among no fewer than 60,000 governmental entities, mostly county and local.

Land: 60,000 Fast-Buck Operators

In the Chicago metropolitan area alone more than a thousand communities have authority to regulate land use, and in general they operate quite independently of each other. Only a few states have laws allowing the state to override local zoning decisions. The yardstick of most local zoning is not even the best long-range interests of the community itself, let alone of the state or nation. The yardstick is what use classification will bring in the most tax dollars *tomorrow*.

Thus, because a junkyard on the outskirts of a community will yield more taxes than a vacant lot, the junkyard automatically gets preference over some possible long-range plan for better use of the vacant land. And only belatedly do citizens wake up to discover their communities are ringed by unsightly junkyards. State and national considerations get even shorter shrift in local planning.

All this may have made some sense, or at least had some legal validity, in bygone days when states were distinctly separate entities. It makes little sense today. In an era when planes cross the country in five hours; when air pollution from one area is palpable hundreds of miles away; when chemicals made in Los Angeles are found in Arctic penguins; and when the management of the Cape Cod seashore may be of vital interest to a vacationing Texan, colonial-era fragmentation of land-use management clearly is inadequate. The resident of Oregon has an inescapable and inalienable concern with what happens to the land in South Carolina, and vice versa, just as more than a century ago a Massachusetts court ruled that everybody in the state had a legal interest in whether one man turned his beach into a gravel pit.

But in no case has even a single state, in more than the sketchiest and most academic way, ever made a comprehensive inventory of its land and taken steps to adapt the land, as a totality, to a plan of optimum use.

Indeed, a federal commission studying management of the nation's shoreline in 1969 queried all thirty-one coastal states (including those on the Great Lakes) and found that most of them were not even conscious that the shoreline was a distinctive entity calling for special administrative consideration.

Logically, in the face of a prospective national population increase of 100 million in the next thirty years, the federal government long since should have come to grips with this massive anachronism. But it hasn't. It has only shadowboxed with the problem. Bedeviled for years by a host of conflicting interests eying the 750 million acres of federal land, Congress in 1965 created a commission to recommend what should be done about this land.

The Public Land Law Review Commission found itself grappling with a gigantic grab-bag. About half the public land is in Alaska. Most of the rest is in the eleven contiguous western states, comprising up to 86 per cent, in the case of Nevada, of the states' areas. This land encompasses every sort of terrain, from swamps to mountains and from deserts to forests. About 450 million acres is under the Department of the Interior's Bureau of Land Management: the remainder of the "public domain" once wide open to settlement and exploitation. Another 187 million acres are national forests, under the supervision of the Department of Agriculture. Some twenty-eight million acres are national parks, under the Department of the Interior. The rest is under thirty other federal agencies.

This is the national preserve, essentially unoccupied in an era when living space has become almost the scarcest of commodities.

Land: 60,000 Fast-Buck Operators

But "national preserve" is misleading in its implication. Only national parks—one per cent of the nation's land area—are dedicated entirely to public use and safe from incursion and alienation. The national forests have an ambiguous status, partly dedicated to public use and partly to commercial exploitation—lumbering, mining, and grazing. Bureau of Land Management land is open to all these incursions, and much of it is subject to sale or exchange simply by presidential order.

The Public Land Law Review Commission was instructed to determine whether all or part of these lands should be disposed of or retained in federal ownership, and under what provisions. If there had been even a skeleton of a national land-use plan, the commission might have fitted disposition of the federal portion into it under some rational design. As it was, the commission had to function in a sort of vacuum, as if the public domain were isolated from the rest of the country, vaguely hypothesizing how its disposition might fit into some yet unformulated scheme.

As a result the conclusions the commission reported advanced no enterprising new plans; essentially they clung to the status quo. While recommending numerous housekeeping reforms, the commission suggested that the bulk of the land simply be retained in federal ownership. The commission paid verbal obeisance to the newly hallowed values of recreation and environmental quality. But it had a nineteenth-century flavor in its reaffirmation of the dedication of the public domain to commercial exploitative interests.

Some of the land, the commission felt, might be sold off for agriculture, and some was plainly needed for the expansion of existing communities and perhaps the development of a few experimental "new cities." Beyond that, the commission returned the whole kit of problems to the lap of Congress.

The Nixon administration has displayed a conspicuous reluctance to come to grips with the national land-use problem. In his July 1969 message to Congress on population problems, discussed in Chapter 3, President Nixon alluded to the need of putting the nation's land to better use. But he left the matter dangling.

Adequate planning [he said] requires that we ask ourselves a number of important questions. Where, for example, will the next 100 million Americans live? If the patterns of the last few decades hold for the rest of the century, then at least three-quarters of the next 100 million persons will locate in highly urbanized areas.

Are our cities prepared for such an influx? The chaotic history of urban growth suggests that they are not, and that many of their existing problems will be severely aggravated by a dramatic increase in numbers.

Are there ways, then, of readying our cities? Alternatively, can the trend toward greater concentration of population be reversed? Is it a desirable thing, for example, that half of all the counties in the United States actually lost population in the 1950's, despite the growing number of inhabitants in the country as a whole? Are there ways of fostering a better distribution of the growing population?

Some have suggested that systems of satellite cities or completely new towns can accomplish this goal. The National Commission on Urban Growth has recently produced a stimulating report on this matter, one which recommends the creation of ten new communities averaging 100,000 people each, and ten new communities averaging at least one million persons.

But the total number of people who would be accommodated even if this plan were implemented is only twenty million—a mere one-fifth of the expected thirty-year increase. If we were to accom-

Land: 60,000 Fast-Buck Operators

modate the full 100 million persons in new communities, we would have to build a new city of 250,000 persons each month from now until the end of the century. . . . Clearly the problem is enormous, and we must examine the alternative solutions very carefully.

In his State of the Union message on January 22, 1970, President Nixon again paid rhetorical respect to the idea of new-city development, but again left the matter dangling. "In particular," he said, "the federal government must be in a position to assist in the building of new cities and the rebuilding of old ones. . . . We must create a new rural environment which will not only stem the migration to urban centers but reverse it."

There were now some two million more Americans than when he first broached the subject. But within six months, according to *U.S. News and World Report* (July 6, 1970), a two-day closed-door White House conference of urban planners, demographers, and other specialists had convinced itself, and President Nixon, that the innovations he had extolled could be avoided.

The principal basis for this conclusion apparently was some revised population projections indicating that the national growth in the next thirty years would not be 100 million but only seventy-million. To a layman this would appear to be a small difference in degree rather than in principle. But it was enough for the group to decide, according to the magazine, that "no amount of money or other federal help could stop the decline of small towns in rural America, and that the government should concentrate rather on improving the planning and development of metropolitan areas."

The conference, the article continued, "showed little confidence in the government's ability to decide where an addi-

37

tional seventy-eight million people were going to work and live," and "Nixon agreed with the general feeling of the group that a program to build new towns at a distance from cities is not a good bet and that efforts along this line should be limited to some experimental towns, mostly of a satellite nature."

The Housing Act of 1970, signed by President Nixon early in 1971, was touted as a major move to finance the development of "new towns." On examination it proved to be considerably less than this.

The law *authorized* expenditures (contingent on appropriations) of $2.9 billion. But most of this was designated for various sorts of urban *renewal* (which tends to decrease housing accommodations rather than increase them). The amount applicable to "new town" development amounted to only a few hundred million dollars. How far this would go in creating "new towns" is suggested by the fact that $500 million will pay for exactly 25,000 typical dwellings at $20,000 each.

So much for dispersing population out of the inoperable megalopolises. So much for using the federal government's numerous available tools—placement of contracts, aid grants, technical assistance, and financing resources—to promote new communities with built-in economic bases that would mitigate big cities' concentrations of air and water pollution and restore to urban cliff dwellers some of the amenities the cave man enjoyed. So much for putting to good use the nation's vast reaches of idle land.

We were still committed to what C. C. Johnson, Jr., administrator of the Department of Health, Education and Welfare's division of environmental protection, called "a pattern of 'progress' that will soon place most of our growing

Land: 60,000 Fast-Buck Operators

population in unmanageable super-cities stretching along the perimeter of the continent, with a vast and empty wasteland in between."

It remained for Senator Henry Jackson of Washington to make an initial, timid approach to a rational land-use policy. He hesitated to fire a salvo directly at the hoary tradition of states' rights under which what happens in New Mexico is presumed to be of no concern to anyone anywhere else, or at the tacit conspiracy of zoning officials with real-estate interests to promote only parochial, self-serving ends.

Instead, he proposed a mild scheme of subsidies for states to engage in coherent land-use planning consonant with standards to be developed within the federal government. The 1970 Congress did little about Senator Jackson's bill. In his February 1971 environmental message to Congress President Nixon advanced the same idea as if it were something new. No action emerged from Congress in 1971 or 1972.

A few months earlier, Mr. Nixon had spoken cautiously again of the desirability of "an approach to a national land-use policy." Another presidential election was in the offing, and it was not prudent to rile the states by suggesting that decisive federal action on the use of such a basic resource as land—considering the mess the states had made of the problem—was as plausible as federal regulation of the use of the air.

But this hypercaution seemed to be several steps behind public opinion. Polls repeatedly showed that a large number of city dwellers would jump at the chance to move to the hinterland.

Again the situation had the earmarks of one in which, if considered reforms were not initiated expeditiously, drastic measures might have to be taken belatedly.

MADMAN IN A LIFEBOAT

"We have to get a new philosophy of values about the land, property rights and man as only one part of the living community," the *New York Times*' James Reston, no radical, wrote in 1970.

And Michael McCloskey, executive director of the Sierra Club, and a belt-and-suspenders conservative in temperament, said flatly that an inescapable item of environmental reform was "to control the use of private land."

Meanwhile people were continuing to die in the megalopolises essentially because of the lack of a national land-use policy. The miser was starving to death in his furnished room while thumbing, beady-eyed, through his effulgent bankbooks.

6

Air Pollution: Half the Cards Are Wild

AIR POLLUTION is a unique problem in that it is the only sort of pollution in which a critical factor is entirely beyond man's control.

A serious air pollution "episode" results from two things: a flow of contaminants into the air, and a static atmospheric "lid" that traps an accumulation of pollutants, perhaps to the point of suffocation.

This is what happened in the Meuse Valley in Belgium in 1930—the first severe air pollution incident in history. Sixty people died.

This is what happened in Donora, Pennsylvania, in 1948, when twenty persons died and 6,000 became ill.

This is what happened in London in 1952: an episode followed by 4,000 deaths over the normal mortality rate. Less serious episodes, but with statistically demonstrable casualties, have occurred since in both London and New York.

Man can avert water pollution almost entirely simply by not allowing contaminants to get into waterways. There are always alternative means of dealing with fluid wastes, such as by dehydrating them in ponds and treating the residue as solid waste. Solid wastes can be recycled, burned, or buried.

But man has only a limited degree of control of air pollution. People have to breathe, and exhale waste gases. Combustion has to take place, and by definition it produces residues. These can be made innocuous only up to a point. Even if all the automobiles in the United States could be rid of their noisome effluents, you would still have 100 million vehicles discharging the ingredients of soda water—carbon dioxide and water. And even these compounds in large quantities can be a problem.

Some scientists foresee the upper atmosphere being permanently altered in as yet unpredictable ways simply by the cumulative carbon dioxide-and-water emissions of the ever-growing world fleet of jet planes. The air thins out rapidly with altitude. Two miles up humans accustomed to normal air have trouble breathing. A few miles higher and the air is so thin it does not behave like air at sea level: alien substances as simple as water may linger for years.

Vagaries of the weather can not only trap air pollution but also *magnify* it.

In the San Bernardino national forest eighty miles east of Los Angeles, ponderosa pines, which "breathe" through particularly sensitive needles, are being killed by smog, even though there are no smog sources nearby. The pines are a mile above sea level. This is twice as high as the common atmospheric lids (formed by an abnormally low layer of cool air) that trap the effluents of hundreds of thousands of cars and other smog sources in the San Bernardino Valley below.

Air Pollution: Half the Cards Are Wild

But what happens is this. Evening breezes coming off the ocean *push* the trapped gases up the side of the San Bernardino Mountains, and in so doing they concentrate them. The result is that the ponderosa pines are subjected to vagrant air pollution densities far higher than the "acceptable" limits in the valley below: if the same densities occurred there, they would be cause for an "alert."

The same thing could happen anywhere in the country, given freak weather factors. The National Weather Service regularly issues advisories of "high air pollution potential" (HAPP) conditions—masses of stagnant air that may cover as much as 250,000 square miles at one time. In recent years HAPP advisories have been issued at the rate of more than one a month. Such a condition was responsible for the New York metropolitan area's scary Thanksgiving week smog episode in 1966.

That a dangerous episode of air pollution can be quite beyond man's control has not yet been conceptually grasped by most people in the United States, or in other countries. They continue to think of the atmosphere as having a fixed absorptive capacity for gaseous wastes, and they approach questions of air pollution control on this basis. The premise is that there is a certain amount of contaminants that can be "safely" emitted into the air of a given locality in a given period.

This is like the old theory that waterways have an "assimilative capacity" for neutralizing wastes that can be taken advantage of without bothering anybody. The trouble is that then you start out with polluted water, and in case of an accident, or the addition of new pollution sources, you are immediately above the "assimilative capacity." You have water that has lost its regenerative capacity and is septic.

With air, this notion of an assimilative capacity is particularly treacherous because of the weather factor. The public, in effect, is playing a poker game under the impression that regular rules apply, whereas actually at least half the cards in the deck are wild—their values are variable and unpredictable. Given the unpredictability of weather conditions and that a certain amount of air pollution is unavoidable, the only sensible policy is to *minimize* every bit of air pollution possible.

With the notable exception of Los Angeles County, where this strategy has been sedulously followed in regard to stationary smog sources (automobiles being under separate federal jurisdiction), the federal government is a long way from effective national air pollution controls of any sort. Its record of action on air pollution has been an egregious one of too little and too late. No one knows how many lives it has cost already or will cost before effective measures are in force.

Air pollution as a community problem made its first appearance in the United States in Los Angeles near the end of World War II.

In 1948 came the Donora catastrophe—at the time not perceived as having any relationship with the problem in Los Angeles.

The following year, in the Los Angeles area, Dr. Arie Haagen-Smit of the California Institute of Technology, established that automobiles were a big source of smog. He demonstrated in the laboratory that sunlight, acting on automobile exhaust fumes—the "photochemical effect"—could transform them into a great collection of different, persistent, and toxic compounds.

Yet it was five years before the automobile industry even

Air Pollution: Half the Cards Are Wild

formed a committee to investigate this problem. And it was 1955 before Congress took formal cognizance of air pollution, in a law authorizing the expenditure of $5 million a year —less than three cents per citizen—for smog research and "technical assistance" to the states. It was 1963 before Congress established federal authority to proceed against interstate air pollution situations (only a handful of which were tackled in the next seven years).

It was 1965, sixteen years after Haagen-Smit's discovery of the link between smog and automobiles, before Congress passed the first law to control car fumes (and this didn't take effect until the 1968 models). And it was 1967 before Congress passed the first comprehensive air pollution control law, which was so indecisive that more than four years later there had not been one ounce of air pollution abatement directly attributable to this law.

From 1967 through 1970—during which time, according to responsible medical judgment, numbers of people died from the effects of air pollution—federal and state officials (with industry obstructing rather than expediting the process) were engaged in a massive paper-shuffling exercise setting up emission standards and delineating jurisdictional areas.

The additional air pollution control act that was signed on the last day of 1970—after ten months of congressional debate—closed some of the regulatory loopholes and streamlined some of the procedures. But even this law—so complex as to defy succinct summary—contained provisions not fully enforceable before 1977. That will be more than thirty years after smog's appearance, a full generation: people who weren't born when smog first shrouded Los Angeles will have children of their own far beyond the diaper stage.

45

The full effects of current automobile fume controls are not scheduled to accrue until 1980, and even these projections are problematical. They are 1970-vintage projections premised on tests of the efficiency of fume control equipment which many experts consider statistically inconclusive, if not meaningless.

Up to 1971 the testing involved only a tiny sampling of cars which, after being taken from the production lines, were allowed to be specially tuned. And even then many of the sample cars did not meet specified levels of fume control: manufacturers were allowed to "average" performances of cars above and below the required levels. Finally, the 25,000-mile and 50,000-mile tests of the control equipment's sustained performance were of necessity based on test-track mileage rather than realistic car use. Independent engineers have observed some quick drop-offs in the equipment's efficiency under the dust, dirt, weather, and neglect of typical car ownership.

Research on alternatives to the standard gasoline engine —propulsion by natural gas, electricity, steam, or whatnot— however successful it may ultimately be, has no bearing on the short-range auto smog problem. If the nongasoline "miracle car" were ready for mass production today, it would take ten years at Detroit's present production rate to replace all the gasoline-engine cars on the road.

And automobiles represent roughly half of the nation's air pollution problem.

Even when all the existing air pollution legislation is in effect, it will still be oriented toward the concept of the atmosphere's having an "assimilative capacity" under which a multitude of pollution sources can be allowed a certain amount of contamination, rather than being required to hold

Air Pollution: Half the Cards Are Wild

their emissions to the technological minimum.

Thus there seems a basis for some scientists' predictions that there will be catastrophic air pollution episodes before the nation really comes to grips with air pollution. And these grim predictions stand entirely apart from the fact that many other nations are acting even less responsibly about air pollution than the United States—while the earth's atmosphere remains an indivisible entity oblivious to national boundaries.

So the net conclusion can only be that with air, as with its other resources, the world is still emulating the madman in the lifeboat.

7

Water Pollution: The Land of Open Sewers

"HERE IS MAN," a philosopher of the 1960's said, "reaching for the moon—and standing knee-deep in sewage...."

Not only is he standing knee-deep in it: he's fighting over it.

A few miles outside Las Vegas, Nevada, on a cleft in the barren desert, a creek called Las Vegas Wash flows into Lake Mead, behind Hoover Dam on the Colorado River, at the rate of some thirty million gallons a day. Most of the flow is treated sewage from Las Vegas. As these words are being written, two of the major governmental entities in the area are vying for title to the sewage.

The area gets its water from the Colorado River. Nevada's Colorado River Commission is insisting that after the water is used, the residue must go back into the river to avoid unduly depleting its flow.

The Nevada Power Company, which supplies the Las Vegas area with electricity, says it must build a new power plant on the outskirts of the city to meet the growing de-

Water Pollution: The Land of Open Sewers

mand. Like all power plants, this one will need large quantities of steam-condensing water. It can't get it from the river, because Nevada's share of the river's flow is already committed.

The refined sewage from Las Vegas Wash seems to be the only answer. So for more than a year the power company had its lawyers combing the statute books to establish that sewage, once discharged from the treatment plant, is in effect up for grabs, and that the Colorado River administrators have no prior claim on it.

Things that happen in the Nevada desert, particularly around Las Vegas, may seem atypical. But today the problem of Las Vegas Wash is the problem of the entire country, and of many foreign countries.

Everyone has seen diagrams of the elementary process formidably called "the hydrologic cycle." Water falls onto the earth in the form of rain and snow. Various things happen to it. At one point it evaporates into the air, to come down again as rain or snow. Evaporation is nature's way of purifying the water, leaving all contaminants behind.

Once that process sufficed. But in the last century man and his uses of water have so proliferated that water is used faster than nature can purify it. A good deal of our water is used several times before it continues on through the natural cycle.

It can be proved by a dizzying array of statistics that at the rate we're using water in the United States now in a few years there won't be enough fresh water to go around—for communities, for industry, for agriculture. The operative word is "fresh." By far the biggest single use of water in the country today is the 50 trillion gallons that industry borrows annually simply for cooling purposes, principally in power

49

plants. It is discharged containing only one pollutant, heat —although that can be as deleterious in some circumstances as chemical pollution.

The nation's essential problem, then, is cleaning up *used* water. There are two ways of doing this. One is by not allowing the water to get dirty. The other is by processing the water to remove such pollution as is unavoidable.

To date we've been a lot more progressive about cleaning up water than about not polluting it in the first place.

Years ago some eastern steel plants began using cleaned-up sewage for boiler-cooling water. At Lake Tahoe, on the California-Nevada line, where the topography necessitates pumping sewage out of a mountain basin, it is cleaned up almost to drinking-water quality and used to irrigate crops across the ridge. In Santee, California, sewage is purified so thoroughly that it ends up as the water in a sparkling series of municipal swimming pools and boating ponds. In Los Angeles—although most residents of the area don't know it —large quantities of purified sewage water are allowed to percolate down through the ground into the aquifer strata that provide much of the area's drinking water.

This is not as horrendous as it sounds. Typical sewage is more than 99 per cent plain water: the contaminants amount to only a few parts per million.

"Primary" sewage treatment consists of allowing heavy materials to settle out. Then "secondary" treatment takes over. This consists typically of the "activated sludge" process. Sewage is churned in big vats where benign bacteria disintegrate most of the contaminants into the basic chemical elements and compounds they were originally. Good secondary treatment removes upward of 85 per cent of the oxygen-demanding contaminants.

Water Pollution: The Land of Open Sewers

Chief among the remaining pollutants, after secondary treatment, are nitrates and phosphates, which are essentially "clean," but which are natural fertilizers that promote the growth of objectionable plant life in waterways where the sewage residues end up.

To get rid of nitrates and phosphates and another stubborn contaminant, salt, requires "tertiary," or third-stage, treatment, generally known as advanced waste treatment. This involves a variety of precipitation and filtering processes. The product of good tertiary treatment is water that is purer than most drinking water. Thus man matches nature's process of evaporation without going to distillation, which is expensive. Eventually tertiary treatment, now practiced in only a few places, will become general. Man will then have duplicated nature on a speeded-up basis. Water will be a regularly recycled commodity, and shortages, actual or prospective, should be a forgotten problem.

We are manifestly a long way from this idyllic day.

All the nation's principal river systems are polluted. The pollution comes from a half-dozen basic sources. The foremost sources are industry, which uses 200 billion gallons of water a day, and municipal sewer systems, which carry away most of the approximately 27 billion gallons a day used by communities. Then there is urban run-off. Some of this goes through storm-drain systems. Some, which once would have been absorbed into the ground, now just sluices off the increasingly large areas of paved and built-up terrain. In both cases, this run-off water is about as dirty as sewage.

There is a large volume of pollution from agriculture: animal wastes, farm chemicals, and irrigation drainage.

Another source, which cannot be discounted in an era

when 200 million tons of gaseous pollutants are going into the skies every year, is fallout pollution precipitated by rain and snow. The presence of lead and mercury in remote lakes has been attributed to this action.

Finally, there is natural pollution: decaying vegetable and animal matter, and particularly silt from natural erosion, which makes waterways murky and precludes normal animal and plant life.

Natural pollution and fallout largely defy measurement. Agricultural pollution is so diffuse that it has been measured only in isolated situations. It has been suggested, however, that it might be comparable in scope to municipal and industrial pollution. There are 500 million farm animals in the country producing ten times as much bodily waste by weight as the human population; and only a fraction of it is systematically treated.

Of some 300,000 manufacturing establishments in the country, about 10,000 account for 90 per cent of industrial water use, using upward of 20 million gallons a year each.

The commonest gauge of water pollution potential is "biological oxygen demand" (BOD), a measure of substances' capacity for depleting water of the free oxygen by which it normally breaks down foreign matter. The nation's manufacturing establishments, according to the Council on Environmental Quality, annually produce 13,100 billion gallons of waste fluids (apart from cooling water) containing 18 billion pounds of suspended solids with a BOD rating of 22 million pounds. This potential load on waterways compares with 7.3 billion BOD pounds from community sewage systems.

Both measurements were before treatment. There are after-treatment measurements on municipal sewage, but a national inventory of industrial discharges was launched only

Water Pollution: The Land of Open Sewers

late in 1970, after years of opposition from industry. There is no evidence that industrial wastes generally receive any more predischarge treatment than municipal wastes.

But if industry has been laggard in treating its wastes, municipalities are equally culpable in principle. The Council on Environmental Quality reported in 1970 that about one-third of the nation's citizens had no sewage service. Another one-third were on systems that did not provide adequate sewage treatment.

Of 13,000 communities with sewage systems, the Federal Water Quality Administration (now incorporated into the Environmental Protection Agency) reported, 1,300 were discharging untreated sewage into rivers, lakes, and the ocean. Another 1,300 communities were providing only "primary" solids-settling treatment. The rest were providing various degrees of secondary treatment, now considered a norm. The FWQA estimated that industrial discharges imposed an oxygen demand on waterways equivalent to the *untreated* sewage of 165 million people. Dr. Barry Commoner, a biologist at Washington University, estimated that by 1980, without radical reforms, the untreated fraction of the nation's municipal sewage alone would contain biological oxygen demand equal to all the free oxygen in the twenty-five major river systems of the country.

The reason for these deficiencies on the part of both industry and municipalities has been a simple reluctance to spend money, combined with apathy and ignorance on the part of the public, which could have brought pressures for bigger expenditures.

Industry traditionally eschews expenditures that do not contribute directly to profits. Among municipal officials, sewage-plant expenditures have a minimum of political appeal: you can get more votes by erecting a statue.

Both industry and municipalities historically have used their political leverage to soft-pedal enforcement of state water pollution laws. Because of state laxity, the federal government moved into the field of water pollution abatement in 1948. The intervening years have brought a series of laws that sounded good but were negated by cumbersome procedures and by sedulous foot-dragging by polluters.

Between 1957 and 1970, under a grant program, the federal government distributed $1.5 billion to help build and expand municipal sewage plants. The subsidies were matched by nearly $5 billion in state and local funds. Sewage treatment was extended to 25 per cent of the nation's population that had been without it. In 1968 federal spokesmen reported that the grants program had helped to improve the quality of 50,000 miles of the nation's three million miles of streams. But continuing pollution is conspicuous, and officials feel that efforts up to now have done no more than offset the annual increases in abatement needs, leaving the previous deficiencies to be dealt with. Estimates of needed industrial and municipal sewage facilities range as high as $100 billion.

It was 1969 before the federal-state water quality standards program—prescribed in the 1965 water pollution law—had advanced far enough for the federal government to begin bringing injunction actions against violators.

In 1970, a little-used provision of the 1899 River and Harbor Act was invoked, requiring that all dischargers of fluid wastes into waterways, except municipal sewage systems, obtain federal permits.

The Water Pollution Control Act of 1972 began a whole new ball game. It authorized the appropriation of $24 billion

Water Pollution: The Land of Open Sewers

over six years, mostly for 75 per-cent-of-cost grants to municipalities for sewage treatment systems; and set up a new federal-state permit program.

Envisioning the elimination of all contaminant discharges into waterways by 1985, the law called for the application of the "best practicable" waste treatment technology by 1977, and the "best available" technology by 1983.

President Nixon vetoed the measure as inflationary. Congress overrode his veto—leaving moot the question of how future Congressional appropriations to implement the law might fare at the hands of Executive budget-parers.

And leaving up in the air also the question of how long it would take the nation, in respect to its water resources, to turn away from the mores of the madman in the lifeboat.

8

Solid Waste: In the Footsteps of the Cave Man

PERHAPS the commonest feature of the environmental crisis is the quest for scapegoats.

There are, of course, some conspicuous *contributors* to environmental degradation. But the blame for their actions rests ultimately with the public that lets them get away with it.

The most pointed evidence of the public's default is the problem of solid waste.

It is hardly up to Washington to take care of anybody's trash. It isn't up to anybody at the state capital. It is plainly a community responsibility. But the record of the nation's communities in this regard is terrible. In general, they have clung tenaciously to the mores of the cave man. Ancient habitations are discovered often through their mounds of trash. Today's civilization, if it were suddenly to be extinguished, could be traced the same way. Except for a few enlightened communities, the prescription for rubbish has

Solid Waste: In the Footsteps of the Cave Man

been: take it to the outskirts of town and dump it. The system worked all right, if your philosophy was out-of-sight-out-of-mind, until about a decade ago. By then communities throughout the country had grown until their borders met. And suddenly we were out of outskirts. Or, if there was any open space left, it was too valuable to be used as a dumping ground.

San Francisco was the first city to sound the alarm. In 1967 it jolted the country with the announcement that, because it was running out of dumping space, it was considering a plan of hauling its refuse 375 miles by train to a desert tract in northeastern California. The program still hadn't jelled four years later. Interim dumping space was located when the rail-haul plan proved too expensive.

But San Francisco, it transpired, was only one of many places in the same bind. New York was hard up for dumping space. Philadelphia, Milwaukee, and Denver looked into rail-haul plans. And many another community came face to face with the question: What are we going to do with our trash?

In part the solid waste "crisis"—the threat that the nation might be engulfed in its own refuse—was a concomitant of the age of affluence. The wave of material wealth and the residues thereof had suddenly bumped the nation's once inconspicuous volume of urban rubbish up to one million tons a day.

Spatially speaking there was no national crisis. A year's rubbish from 10,000 people will cover an acre of ground seven feet deep. But there are millions of acres out in the great open spaces where all the nation's trash could be deposited, neatly, for centuries. The problem simply was the economic one of moving rubbish to feasible disposal areas.

Economics was the magic word. What the public was discovering was that the cost of adequate trash removal, along with everything else, had gone up and that the job could no longer be done for the $2 or $3 a month per household that people were used to paying. (Federal officials, in a 1968 survey, found that the average annual expenditure on trash service was $6.80 per capita—$5.40 for collection and $1.40 for final disposition.)

But the question of what *was* a reasonable and necessary charge for proper rubbish disposal uncovered a fiscal and administrative mare's-nest.

Most cities have some sort of municipal rubbish service, at least for households. In some places the work is performed by a city department and city employees. In other places it is contracted out to private franchisers. Either way, there is no uniformity to its financing. In some communities, surveys have shown, the service is performed at cost, and householders are billed accordingly; in others at a profit or at a loss, with the difference going into, or being taken out of, general tax funds. Few citizens have ever bothered to find out what goes on in this regard in their communities. The system, or lack of system, is an open invitation to fund-juggling, either "honest" internal fund-juggling from one municipal account to another, or external fund-juggling involving larceny, graft, and payoffs. Loose money like this always attracts the underworld, and it is no coincidence that trash collection in many places has been permeated with racketeers.

Once again, in the absence of definitive state and local action on a widespread problem, the federal government was impelled to intervene.

In 1965 a solid waste program was set up in the Depart-

Solid Waste: In the Footsteps of the Cave Man

ment of Health, Education and Welfare (ending up, in 1970, as part of the new Environmental Protection Agency). It perked along for five years on modest budgets of no more than $15 million a year, concentrating on fact-finding and financing research projects on ways of dealing with solid waste. It also handed out grants to most of the states to stimulate comprehensive solid-waste planning.

"Half the communities in the country with populations of 2,500 or more," reported the program's first director, Wesley Gilbertson, "are not doing even a minimally acceptable job of solid waste collection and disposal."

Most of the nation's trash is just dumped, and a small part of it is incinerated, although this leaves quantities of ash and other unburnables that have to be dumped also.

Federal surveys indicated that 94 per cent of the approximately 14,000 city dumps were unsatisfactory from the standpoint of health and pollution, as were 75 per cent of the three hundred municipal incinerators.

The nation's annual solid waste load was analyzed as follows:

	MILLION TONS
Residential, commercial and institutional rubbish (collected: 190, uncollected: 60)	250
Industrial wastes	110
Mineral wastes (mining, industrial processing, etc.)	1,700
Agricultural wastes	2,280
Total	4,340

The handling of this by the prevailing unsatisfactory methods, federal experts estimated, costs the country $4.5 billion every year, or about $1 a ton. Thus, any improvements that can be made promise, along with more agreeable results, large-scale national economies.

There are only three things that can be done with refuse: salvage it, burn it, or bury it.

Anyone who has ever looked at the problem has been intrigued with the possibilities of salvage. Sizable quantities of copper, lead, aluminum, glass, and paper are regularly recycled. But as soon as you get into cheaper materials, such as the steel of which "tin" cans are made, recycling becomes economically marginal. It's cheaper to get brand-new material than to mess around with reprocessing. Although the environmental crisis inspired widespread citizen efforts to reduce the quantity of solid waste by collecting old bottles and cans for recycling, the value of these activities has been psychological rather than substantial.

Bottle and can makers and users went along with the recovery idea as a public relations gesture. But it is doubtful that the campaigns have recovered their costs. In any case they involve only an insignificant fraction of the solid waste volume.

Although public attention has centered on containers and packaging because they are highly visible, packaging of all types constitutes less than 15 per cent of residential-commercial-industrial waste. And the amount of collected urban waste, which increased from 2.75 pounds per capita in 1920 to five pounds in 1970, is projected to rise to eight pounds by 1980. This is a ten-year increase of nearly 50 per cent, or three times as much as could be offset by the complete abolition of packaging.

Solid Waste: In the Footsteps of the Cave Man

Hundreds of ideas have been explored for disposing of waste in ways other than dumping. They range from using it for fuel to chemically treating waste paper so it can be fed to cattle. As yet, none of these has proved economic. A perpetual will-o'-the-wisp has been the idea of grinding up rubbish into compost. At least a dozen elaborate ventures of this sort have failed because there just isn't a market for that much compost.

As I pointed out earlier, the destruction of exhaustible resources like metals is foolish. But that is the way the prevailing price system works.

An alternative to depletion-oriented pricing that various governmental entites have been discussing is the imposition of arbitrary surcharges on products, calculated either to encourage recycling or at least to offset eventual disposal costs. The prospects of this strategy seem problematical.

But even extensive recycling, if it is achieved, will not eliminate the question of sound solid waste management: the collection of refuse and the disposal of that portion of it that is not reusable.

Accordingly the federal program has been directed dually at developing recycling possibilities and at bringing order out of the chaos of present waste handling through numerous experimental pilot projects designed as constructive examples. One avenue of improvement is to coordinate waste handling on a regional basis rather than the prevalent highly fragmented and inefficient municipal pattern. Federal officials estimated in 1968 that communities needed to spend $835 million a year for five years to bring existing facilities up to par.

In Los Angeles County, covering 5,000 square miles with a population of seven million, seventy collection stations assemble refuse and deposit it in "sanitary landfill" sites (layers of compacted rubbish covered by layers of compacted dirt) in a number of canyons. Some valuable real estate has been created this way.

In some flat sections of the country, small recreational mountains have been built from trash covered with dirt. Not all localities have either the topography or drainage characteristics suitable for landfill operations. But in most communities there are chances to effect big improvements in the present nationwide expanse of ugly dumps and malodorous incinerators.

By 1970 the solid waste problem had gained enough recognition that Congress voted to expand the federal program to $463 million over the ensuing three years. Illustrating the familiar gap between authorization and funding, Congress's proposal of a $172 million outlay for the fiscal year 1971–72 shrank to a proposed $19,289,000 in the administration's budget.

But in few places in the country, as of 1971, were there any indications of movement at the crux of the solid waste problem: the relationship between citizens and their own city halls. It was an illuminating if depressing commentary on where the responsibility for the environmental crisis ultimately lay.

9

The Big Myth: "We Can't *Afford* to Be Clean..."

THE BIGGEST MYTH beclouding the cause of environmental reform is the notion that it's something we may not be able to afford.

It doubtless is true, as the anvil chorus of polluters and exploiters irrelevantly chants, that to gold-plate the countryside and transform all the rivers into distilled water would be inordinately expensive. But that is a very remote issue that can be worried about after we get things just reasonably clean. And the most expansive estimates of what a reasonably clean environment would cost are peanuts in terms of national wealth.

The most authoritative and comprehensive estimate currently available is that set forth by the Federal Council on Environmental Quality in its 1972 annual report, based on studies by its own experts, by the Environmental Protection Agency and by leading industry sources.

Because pollution control projects often span several years

from inception to activation, the estimate was made for the decade from 1971 to 1980, when the nation's current pollution abatement effort is scheduled to have gained full impetus.

The estimate covered capital investment, depreciation and annual operating costs, to government, industry and citizens, necessary to meet prescribed standards as of 1972.

The total for all the basic types of pollution came to $287.1 billion for the decade, divided as follows:

Air pollution	$ 106.5 billion
Water pollution	87.3
Solid waste	86.1
Other*	7.2

*includes airplane noise, radiation protection, and reclamation of surface-mined land

The situation in 1980, assuming the needed facilities are installed, the Council projected as this: There will be $77 billion worth of facilities "in place" (compared to $28.4 billion worth in 1970); additional capital investment will be proceeding at a rate of $9.5 billion a year; and the aggregate annual cost, including capital investment, operation and depreciation, will be $33.3 billion.

The total of $287.1 billion averages out to $28.7 billion a year. This is equivalent to less than 3 per cent of the nation's annual output of goods and services—the Gross National Product—which is now running about $1,000 billion—a *trillion* dollars—a year.

That $28.7 billion a year averages out to about $140 per citizen per year. This is a pertinent figure, since even governmental and industrial costs eventually come from citizens,

The Big Myth: "We Can't *Afford* to Be Clean. . . ."

the only basic source of money in the country.

Actually, the out-of-pocket cost to the average citizen will be far less, for several reasons.

One reason is that one of the largest items in that $287.1 billion, $61 billion of the $106.5 billion for air pollution, represents what automobile buyers (a special group) will be paying, as part of cars' list prices, for fume-control equipment.

Secondly, most of the $86.1 billion item for solid waste represents what citizens are paying already for trash collection and disposal.

In fact, when we subtract from all categories of that $287.1 billion total moneys that, as of 1970, were being spent anyway, the *additional* outlays that the pollution abatement program will cost the nation come to only $182.5 billion for the decade, the CEQ said, or only $18.25 billion a year—considerably less than $100 per citizen.

Finally, we shouldn't forget—going back to that all-inclusive projection of $28.7 billion a year—that *unabated* pollution is costing the nation a great deal of money now.

The CEQ estimates that air pollution is costing some $16 billion a year in medical expenses and damage to materials and crops. Water pollution, according to an estimate by National Wildlife Federation economists, is costing over $12 billion a year. Those two items alone approximately match the $28.7 billion the nation is being asked to expend.

Beyond those two items, excessive airplane noise costs countless billions a year in diminished property values. (Damage suits against the city of Los Angeles for its airport noise aggregated, in 1972, some $5 billion.) Haphazard, inefficient dumping of refuse (the national load runs 1 million tons a day) probably entails losses of more billions in property and materials values.

So that, in reality, the large-sounding expense of pollution abatement has the potential of producing savings to the nation of a far greater dollar amount.

The CEQ did not deny that some individual industrial establishments might be hit hard by new pollution control requirements. But, the Council noted, over 10,000 commercial and industrial establishments go out of business every year in the normal attrition of our competitive economy.

What about the effect of pollution control requirements on employment? The Council concluded that this impact would be very small.

"Manufacturing is the major segment of the economy affected," it reported. "It accounts for 20.2 million employees out of a total labor force of 84.2 million, or 24 per cent.

"Manufacturing industries with the most intensive pollution problems account for almost 28 per cent of total manufacturing employment. Therefore the employment in those industries that will be impacted to any significant degree by pollution control amounts to about 7 per cent of the current work force. And of that, only a small percentage will be in those plants which would be so severely hit as to face possible layoffs."

Getting down to specifics, the cost of water pollution control on a new industrial plant seldom runs more than 10 per cent of the total construction cost. Air pollution control equipment, according to various federal estimates, is closer to 5 per cent. The cost of community sewage treatment facilities averages out at around $40 per capita. That sounds

The Big Myth: "We Can't *Afford* to Be Clean...."

like an uncomfortable tax bite if imposed in a single year. But such facilities customarily are amortized over at least a twenty-year period, which would bring the levy down to $8 a year for a family of four. There is extensive additional evidence that the costs of pollution control are not inordinate.

A 1970 federal survey of coal-fired electric generating plants indicated that control of soot—one of the chief pollutants of such plants—ranged between .7 per cent and 2 per cent of power production costs. Since these are only half of the final cost of electric service, this pollution control would increase the typical household electric bill of $120 a year by somewhere between 42 cents and $1.20. The study did not cover two other common power plant pollutants, sulphur dioxide and oxides of nitrogen, but even if these represented a tripling of pollution control expense, the total obviously would be far from an impossible burden on the nation.

Another federal study in 1970 indicated that the cost of obviating thermal pollution by installing various kinds of cooling systems for the condensing water in power plants could cost consumers as little as five cents a month, and with the most expensive conceivable method no more than fifty cents a month.

Still another gauge of pollution control economics related to specific quantities of pollution is the case of the new Mohave power plant in southern Nevada, built by the Southern California Edison Company for a consortium of electric utilities. The coal-fired plant cost about $200 million. Of this, about $10 million was for pollution control equipment. The equipment was designed to eliminate 96 per cent of soot emissions, leaving a discharge of about one ton an hour. Subsequently a state regulation was adopted requiring 98.6

per cent soot control, limiting the discharge to one-half ton of soot per hour. The power company estimated in 1970 that the modifications necessary to meet this requirement might cost an additional $4 million. That would still leave the pollution-control component at only 7 per cent of the total plant cost, there being no water pollution control expense in this situation.

This discussion has centered on power plants because they are the most uniform of industrial facilities in terms of processes, products, and equipment, and hence are the ones on which the most comprehensive figures are available. But pollution control costs in other industries are not inordinately different.

Much of the $1,000 billion in the gross national product represents "fat"—effort that is of very limited value in terms of national economic welfare, such as the production of war planes and bombs that will be quickly destroyed. Other billions of the GNP represent redundant luxuries, such as the production and distribution costs of assorted brands of toothpaste and lipstick.

The man-hours devoted to such activities can, in terms of economic dynamics, easily be diverted to environmental improvement, if the public wants, at no sacrifice to the national economy. The same thing applies in terms of the federal budget. At the time we were quibbling about spending millions on environmental improvements (it transpired in 1970), more than a billion dollars was going out in cost overruns on one military plane of questionable value.

Three numbers to remember in any discussion of national pollution abatement costs are 1,000, 200, and 20. One thousand billion dollars is the national economic bank account

The Big Myth: "We Can't *Afford* to Be Clean...."

against which any such expenditures can, in effect, be drawn. Two hundred is the number of million citizens among whom any national expenditure is, directly or indirectly, divided. And twenty years is the period over which the costs of most pollution control equipment can be spread.

One big fallacy the "we can't afford it" people wittingly or unwittingly are constantly advancing is the idea that environmental reform involves some sort of one-fell-swoop irreversible commitment that we should be very wary of. This is nonsense. Environmental reform is proceeding on a thousand simultaneous fronts and movement on each of these fronts is the result of a multitude of separate commitments, chiefly financial ones. Nobody is being called upon to make an all-inclusive, one-time decision.

Nobody can commit the nation to that $105 billion six-year outlay the Council on Environmental Quality predicated. It will come about only as the result of a complex of decisions by many units of government, countless segments of industry, and thousands of communities.

What everyone *is* being called upon to do—and what the polluters and despoilers in various devious ways are trying to thwart—is simply to espouse environmental reform as an important element in decision-making and policy-making.

Within this framework there are innumerable built-in brakes to forestall any real impairment of the nation's economy.

So the notion that environmental reform *per se* may be something we can't afford is nothing but a false reason for inaction.

10

The States: How to Stack a Pollution Board

THE FEDERAL GOVERNMENT can make policies and laws on environmental problems, but implementation of them ultimately depends on the states.

There are 300,000 industrial establishments in the country, at least 10,000 sizable communities, about three million farms, and many another potential pollution source. The federal government cannot conceivably police them. Surveillance is possible only at the state level. Up to now the states' record in maintaining environmental standards has, on the face of it, been anywhere from poor to awful, depending on one's location and sensitivities.

Why have the states been ineffectual?

The underlying reason, of course, has been public apathy and ignorance. But beyond this has been the political and economic power of polluters.

Legislative bodies—state, county, and city—can pass laws against pollution and other environmental evils. But vested

The States: How to Stack a Pollution Board

interests in pollution—industrial establishments, farmers, counties, cities—have many ways of negating such regulation.

Sometimes such laws are made for show, without any teeth. They sternly proscribe environmental abuse, but contain only wrist-slapping penalties. Or they prescribe stiff penalties but conveniently omit adequate enforcement machinery. Or they have the bold words, the penalties, and the enforcement machinery, but there are insufficient appropriations to make it all work.

Or, if all these loopholes are plugged, enforcement procedures may be so cumbersome that it is difficult to get corrective action.

Finally, the best regulatory structure can be neutralized by officials who simply drag their feet in doing their jobs because they are afraid of offending influential polluters.

The whole scenario has been played out time and again at federal water pollution abatement hearings that have been held throughout the country. These have been the principal occasions, under existing law, where it has been possible to shine a spotlight of reality behind the pompous façades of the states' faltering pollution control apparatus.

At a typical hearing, for instance, it will be brought out that the XYZ Company is polluting a river horrifically. The federal examiner will then turn to the responsible state officials and ask, "Why is this going on?"

The state officials then more often than not launch into long, windy excuses and rationalizations.

"We've been after the XYZ Company for years," they will say. "They admit they're polluting. But they have a tough problem. It took a lot of engineering studies to figure out how to solve it."

(Note the speciousness of the story already. The XYZ Company, we are given to believe, is manufacturing a unique product by some esoteric processes producing effluents posing a need for control equipment that has never arisen in that particular industry before.)

"The corrective equipment is costing them a lot of money," the state officials will continue, "and installing it involves a lot of shut-down time.

"The company has been very cooperative. They've agreed on a clean-up program. . . . Sure, they're three years behind schedule on it . . . but they say they'll have everything straightened out in a couple of more years.

"We're confident that they're doing the best they can. And you can be sure we're watching that situation closely."

The trouble is that when you get through all that verbiage, the water or air or whatnot is just as dirty as it was five years before—in a period when the nation is supposed to have been moving in the direction of environmental improvement. As one federal water pollution official put it: "Excuses butter no trout."

If this sort of whining apologia for the status quo came up only occasionally it might have some plausibility. But it has been the standard song and dance. One time it's an industrial plant and its troubles. The next time it's a municipality, with a tale of woe about how short it is of money. (Was there ever a municipality with a *surplus?*) Another time it's a cattle-feeding lot, telling how hard it is to get rid of manure.

The net result is: no action. And so pollution has gone on.

Federal water pollution abatement actions involving states, industry, and municipalities started as far back as 1957 are still pending. In air pollution, apart from automobiles, the federal-state regulatory program had just reached

The States: How to Stack a Pollution Board

the point early in 1972 where all fifty states under the law were due to submit proposed ambient air standards and enforcement plans for federal approval.

Some light is beginning to show at the end of the tunnel with tightened federal ground-rules. But they face inertia at the state level. Evidence of the sluggishness in most states was brought out in a nationwide study by the *New York Times* in 1970 of the composition of the state boards that are supposed to regulate air and water pollution. These customarily are unpaid, part-time panels of gubernatorially appointed citizens, often supplemented by some key state officials. The boards generally are charged with setting and enforcing air and water pollution standards, and therefore are pivotal in the national movement toward environmental reform.

In thirty-five of the fifty states, the survey found, such boards are "stacked" (although the *Times* eschewed use of that word) with representatives of vested interests in pollution, or with allies of these interests in state officialdom, such as state directors of agriculture and industrial development.

In only seven states were pollution boards found free of such built-in conflicts of interest. These states were Florida, Hawaii, Kansas, Massachusetts, New Mexico, Vermont, and Virginia.

The other eight states get along, significantly, without such boards, dealing with pollution entirely through full-time state agencies. These states are Alaska, Arizona, Illinois, Maryland, New Jersey, New York, Rhode Island, and Washington.

The absence of "stacked" regulatory boards proved no guarantee of environmental perfection. There isn't a state without pollution problems. But the thrust of the findings was that there is manifestly a better chance for improvement when there are not built-in conflicts of interest—and this was seldom the case. And there was obvious correlation between states with the most heavily "stacked" boards and conspicuously poor air and water conditions.

The systematic influence of polluting interests at state capitals was indicated in the uniformity of the laws creating the regulatory boards. In all thirty-five of the "stacked" board states, appointments were made a responsibility of the governor, a key pressure point for political favoritism. More often than not the laws prescribe categories of activity that are to be represented on the boards: two members from industry, one from agriculture, two from municipalities, etc. Grudgingly one or two seats on a board of eight or ten members might be earmarked by statute for "the public," and in rare cases, one or two seats for the field of conservation.

The roster of big corporations—often ones with pollution records—represented on such boards reads like an abbreviated blue book of American industry. And the recurrent representation of certain corporations on boards suggested systematic efforts to infiltrate the regulatory structure.

For instance, late in 1970 the United States Steel Company, repeatedly a defendant in pollution proceedings in several states, had executives on the air pollution boards in Alabama and Utah. Bethlehem Steel and National Steel had employees on Indiana's air and water pollution boards.

Other metal concerns had a prominent part in pollution policy-making and enforcement among the states. The Anaconda Company, defendant in a major Montana pollution suit, had an executive on the air pollution board in Kentucky. An Anaconda lawyer was on the water board in Utah.

The States: How to Stack a Pollution Board

And the former head of an Anaconda subsidiary was chairman of Montana's water pollution board. A Reynolds Metals man was on the Alabama water pollution commission. An Aluminum Company of America lawyer was an industry representative on North Carolina's pollution board (one of a number of dual-purpose state air and water pollution control agencies). And a staff doctor of the company was chairman of Iowa's air pollution control commission.

And so it went—the lead industry, the chemical industry, the paper industry, the mining industry—all nominally helping to control the pollution their industries were helping to create.

The hoary rationale for staffing such state boards with representatives of polluting interests is that they provide needed "expertise." This is pious twaddle. The expertise manifestly is available whether the possessors have seats on boards or not. The expertise argument was flatly rejected by the heads of both the federal air pollution and the water pollution agencies.

David Dominick, federal water quality commissioner, said:

"Where a statutory board has responsibility as part of state government to establish standards for pollution abatement, the public is ill served to have representatives of private vested interests passing judgment on such regulation. There's enough expertise in the public sector where no conflicts of interest would occur. The whole board should represent the public."

And Dr. John Middleton, director of the National Air Pollution Control Administration, said "I think boards should represent disciplines that bear on air pollution rather than economic interests. The pattern of one or two seats on a board being earmarked for the public doesn't make any sense. All the members of the board should represent the public."

The administrator of the new Environmental Protection Agency, William D. Ruckelshaus, in his first communication with the governors of the fifty states, sent them a copy of the *Times* report, saying:

"The article suggests that in some states pollution control boards are comprised heavily of representatives of the sources of the pollution the boards are designed to regulate.

"It is imperative that the men and women who sit on these boards—and who are empowered to set and implement reasonable standards of pollution abatement—be influenced only by the general public interest and not by any special interests. The credibility of our efforts at every level to restore environmental conditions rests on our ability to pursue a rigorously independent course toward a clean and healthy environment."

The federal government then had no way of altering such boards except through subtle pressures. (The 1972 water pollution control law declared ineligible for state water board membership anyone receiving "a substantial portion" of his income from a discharger of fluid waste.)

A follow-up survey by the *Times* late in 1971 produced signs of some movement toward rectifying the situation Ruckelshaus deplored.

The number of states with either air or water pollution boards whose memberships reflected polluting interests had dropped from thirty-five to thirty-two during the year. Alabama and Montana joined the ranks of states with boards structured to exclude bias. Connecticut joined states such as

The States: How to Stack a Pollution Board

New Jersey and Illinois that dispensed with part-time citizen panels and placed pollution control in the hands of full-time professional state agencies.

In a few states there were signs of tenacious adherence to the status quo, and even retrogression. Tennessee replaced its nine-member water pollution board, on which industry and municipalities had two seats each, with a seven-member board with only one seat each for industry and municipalities. The state air pollution board nominally was replaced also, but representation of special-interest groups was substantially retained. From the industry standpoint, the changes worked out like a game of musical chairs.

On the air pollution board, industry retained three seats, while the public at large remained with no specified representation. Employees of DuPont and the Bowaters Southern Paper Corporation lost seats; a Monsanto representative stayed on; and an Aluminum Company of America man was added, along with a local industrialist. In the revamping of the water board, DuPont and Eastman employees were dropped, but a Bowaters man was added.

Arkansas increased the representation of industry on its combination air-water board. It enlarged the panel—which already included a Monsanto employee—from eight to ten members, to include seats for a representative of the mining industry and the director of the state geological commission (who naturally would be oriented toward mining interests). To the mining-industry seat, an employee of the Aluminum Company of America was appointed.

Overall, however, Ruckelshaus called the trend "encouraging."

"Governors seem to be responding to this problem very well, and should be encouraged by their constituents," he commented. "I've found in the past year that there is rampant mistrust of governmental institutions at every level. The only way to overcome this is to operate as openly as possible, and to eliminate any real or apparent conflict of interest, so that people can trust the decisions of these boards."

But it also was obvious that much more time would have to pass before, in many states, real achievements in pollution control would replace the lip service, inertia, and "stacking" that had contributed in a large way to the environmental crisis.

11

Industry: "Trust Everybody— But Cut the Cards..."

A MAJOR PART of the Environmental Revolution is a revolution in American industry.

The change can be summarized quite simply: where industry traditionally has ignored environmental values, it must now take them seriously into account. This is the dictum of the Environmental Revolution and, as simple as it is, it has caused much confusion among the public and among people in industry.

In attempts to find a convenient scapegoat, the environmental crisis has given birth to a great new demonology about industry: industry and its handmaiden, technology, are responsible for environmental deterioration.... This is an inevitable result of the capitalist system.... The managers of industry are heartless fiends....

Those notions, of course, are nonsense.

The left-wing arm-wavers who blame all pollution on industry seem to forget that every time they go to the bathroom or drive a car, they are contributing to the pollution total.

Environmental degradation is not a distinctive characteristic of capitalism. Pollution is just as bad in Soviet Russia, and for the same nondialectical reason: blind dedication to production at the expense of human amenities.

But the greatest fallacy in the new demonology is the implication that industry is something separate from the fabric of society. Of course it is not. The people who man industry are the people who live next door, with the same ideals, consciences, and frailties. General Motors is not the creature of a little group of willful men: it is the property of 350,000 stockholders. Perhaps they have mismanaged it from an environmental standpoint. If so, one has only to look around at the rest of the country to see that they have a lot of company.

The reason for industry's historic neglect of environmental values also is very simple.

The basic legal responsibility of the management of any corporation is to make money for shareholders. Any activity that does not contribute to that objective is legally challengeable. One thing that is especially challengeable is "nonproductive" expenditures. Expenditures for pollution control and environmental niceties have traditionally been regarded as nonproductive and therefore kept to a minimum.

There is only one qualification to corporate management's legal responsibility to make money. That is the implicit proviso that it be done within the framework of the law. The goal of profit-making is not legal ground for committing murder or even for spitting on the sidewalk.

But until quite recently there has been neither strong national sentiment for environmental preservation nor anything approaching a coherent body of laws to cover it. Pollu-

Industry: "Trust Everybody—but Cut the Cards..."

tion control started on the local level with the ancient "smoke ordinances." Since then it has been developing as a sketchily enforced patchwork of local, state, and national regulations.

Industry may be criticized for having obstructed the development of meaningful ground rules, which in general it has systematically done. But there is a historic rationale for that. Free enterprise traditionally resisted *all* regulation. If it hadn't, it might have succumbed long since to the endless army of would-be regulators. In the absence of comprehensive environmental regulation, and in the context of competition, industry had to write its own ground rules, against an amorphous bench-mark of public tolerance—and these ground rules quite overtly slighted pollution control.

The essence of revolution is changing the rules in the middle of the game.

This is a very alien, un-American thing.

But it is implicit and inescapable in the Environmental Revolution. And it has been understandably traumatic to industry.

There are sweeping and sometimes ill-conceived public pressures for legislative and administrative reforms. Growing out of these are heavy pressures for industry expenditures for pollution control and environmental enhancement. Finally, there are exhortations from many quarters that industry develop a "social conscience" of the sort that presumably would have averted today's conditions.

Industry, not being the homogeneous thing the name implies, but a vast diversity of activities and viewpoints, has responded in many different ways. Many corporations have recognized that it is, inescapably, a new era and are moving, at various speeds, to mend their fences. Some obviously mistake the Environmental Revolution for a passing fad that can be assuaged by flimflam, by advertising and propaganda lip service to reform and misrepresenting the efforts being exerted.

There is "Chinese bookkeeping," in which the expense of normal process changes is logged up to "pollution control." There is the numbers game in which big figures for pollution control outlays are presented entirely out of context in relation to companies' capital outlays, revenues, and profits. There is the forked-tongue tactic, in which a devout polluter extolls the one little corner of its empire that is clean. There have even been slick, four-color, full-page magazine pictures of "cleaned up" rivers that were nowhere near a company's plant.

Some mossback executives are still prating nineteenth-century clichés, saying that pollution is the inevitable price of progress, that abatement of pollution is technologically impossible or prohibitively expensive. The threnody is reminiscent of the vehement arguments advanced against the abolition of child labor and the institution of the eight-hour day, minimum wages, workmen's compensation, and unionism—the tired plaint that "it can't be done." These contentions, as some previous chapters have tried to show, don't hold water.

Some quarters of industry are still plying the old stratagem of playing off the states against the federal government—on the one hand asking for "uniform" national regulations for the sake of competitive equality, and in the next breath insisting that regulations be tailored to "local conditions." This kind of double-dealing, in the present climate of opinion, won't work either.

Industry: "Trust Everybody—but Cut the Cards..."

The most prevalent misunderstanding is the notion that you can have a revolution without anyone getting hurt or without any toes being stepped on. Sweeping revisions in our standards of environmental quality inevitably mean that those tied to the old standards are affected.

Lamentation is widespread that the demands of the environmental revolution will force some concerns into bankruptcy. To date, the lamentation in general has been far more perceptible than figures to back it up. Unquestionably there will be some "hardship" cases. Many have appeared already —the obsolete, polluting installations that are the "sole support" of some communities.

Of such situations, there are some truisms to be cited. One is that our economic system by definition does not promise anyone a living in a particular situation in perpetuity. Neither the system nor nature offers any guarantees against bankruptcy or physical disaster. Enterprises go to the wall all the time. Individuals are forced to recast their lives after hurricanes and droughts.

But an industrial establishment that will be bankrupted by the cost of pollution controls is an establishment that, by definition, is surviving by polluting. This is not calculated to wring sympathy either from competitive industry or from the public. The "hardship" cases are, if the too seldom used rule of reason is applied, self-liquidating problems. If pollution could be kept entirely within a community, it would be that community's option to live with it. But that is rarely the case. The pollution usually extends at least to the regional or state level, and if this is so, the disruption of a community through the enforced shutdown of a plant should be dealt with on a state or regional basis. The unemployment of a few hundred people should not prove insurmountable to any state or region: it is a problem that is being dealt with in other contexts all the time.

On the other hand, the hardship of a small group of people has never been allowed to override the interests of the nation as a whole. The emphasis on such problems in connection with environmental reform is an appeal to emotion rather than to logic.

The idea that industry should develop a "social conscience" in regard to environment not only is sound but it is inevitable in the present climate of public opinion. Industry can't help doing it.

What is fallacious is any thought that "social conscience" can function as a substitute for governmental regulation. It can be a valuable adjunct to regulation and will make the task of regulation that much easier. But, in a free economy, to have hundreds of thousands of entrepreneurs each custom-tailoring for himself a concept of just what is in the public interest environmentally would be anarchic. That is, indeed, exactly what we *have* had—and what has produced the present environmental crisis.

The alternative approach is epitomized in one of W. C. Fields's trenchant commentaries on humanity: "Trust everybody—but cut the cards. . . ."

On both sides of the Environmental Revolution, among the supporters and the opponents, there are suggestions that it implies the doom of free enterprise.

There seems to me no basis for this conclusion at all. What is implied in the Environmental Revolution are more restraints on laissez-faire, which has been undergoing limitation, in the name of the general welfare, for centuries. A new set of mores is being imposed. But what they add up to is

Industry: "Trust Everybody—but Cut the Cards . . ."

more uniform ground rules to eliminate the unfair advantages that accrued to the unscrupulous or the unthinking in direct proportion to their disregard of environmental values.

In this light the new ground rules will enhance the competitive structure rather than impair it. There is nothing in the theory of free-enterprise capitalism that says it operates better in filth than in a clean environment. "If socialism comes to this country," Phillip Berry, president of the militant Sierra Club but also a conservative lawyer, said in 1970, "it will come because business failed in its responsibilities to the environment, its responsibilities to the future, and in a very real sense in its responsibilities to itself."

12

Government: Rebuilding the One-Hoss Shay

THE ENVIRONMENTAL crisis is the result of two hundred years of neglect. Rehabilitation of the environment depends primarily on governmental action, particularly federal action. The Environmental Revolution demands an overhaul in both mechanisms and governmental concepts that go back to the nation's early days.

The state level is vital in *executing* rehabilitative policies. But to avoid the chaos of fifty different ball games, basic policies and ground rules have to be formulated at the national level.

This process so far has been agonizingly slow. One reason is that environmental quality has not yet been accorded the paramount position it deserves in national priorities. Up to now, federal expenditures on environment have been trifling, on the order of one per cent of the national budget—in the same bracket as outlays for foreign aid, the space program, and subsidies to farmers. By contrast, it is recognized as

Government: Rebuilding the One-Hoss Shay

sound economics for individuals to spend 25 per cent of their income for their abode.

Politics is "the art of the possible," or the art of accommodation. But environmental problems have been manifestly the victims rather than the beneficiaries of accommodative maneuvers. The Lyndon Johnson administration produced a lot of impressive environmental rhetoric, along with a number of good deeds, but could not get down to practicalities enough to do anything about the filthy Potomac River running right past the White House door.

The same ambivalence has characterized the Nixon administration. President Nixon spoke brave words about attacking water pollution, but for the initial year of the attack recommended only a $250-million appropriation for sewage-treatment subsidies, when the national consensus—as ultimately enacted by Congress—was that $800 million was needed. In the same breath, in 1971, Mr. Nixon put forward a sweeping environmental improvement program, while assuring industrialists that the government would not be too tough on them about cleaning up their pollution.

Even worse obstacles to environmental improvement are the archaic operations of a Congress still trying to handle twenty-first-century problems with the rituals of the Andrew Jackson era.

An environmental proposal placed in the congressional machinery may end up in any of a score of standing committees, where its fate rests on the parochial whims of a few individuals. Even before full committee consideration, a bill is subject to the caprices of a raft of subcommittees. Somebody counted 250 subcommittees that concern themselves with urban questions alone. Even after there is committee concurrence, and approval by the Senate and House, there is the process of reconciling the two chambers' versions, during which time every detail may be debated all over again. The democratic process does not require so much palaver, and the environmental exigencies we are confronting won't permit it.

A classic case was the so-called Water Quality Act of 1970, which was not all the name implied but dealt chiefly with oil spills. This measure rattled around for two years in the labyrinth of congressional machinery, even though there was substantial agreement from the outset that oil spills had to be regulated. The haggling was over the extent of responsibility (mainly in terms of dollars) that should be imposed. The final result was the setting of a maximum of $14 million liability for an oil spill—roughly 5 per cent of the amount of money the oil industry takes in in *one day.*

In February 1970 President Nixon proposed packages of new legislation to deal with air pollution and water pollution. An air pollution law finally was ratified ten months later. The water pollution proposals did not get beyond token committee hearings in the 1970 session. Senate and House deliberations over markedly different versions of a water pollution bill dragged on through 1971, and well into the 1972 session had not been reconciled in conference committee.

This sort of creaky, deliberate operation is not good enough in an era when, on the word of responsible scientists, a disastrous air pollution episode or a lethal incident of water pollution easily could occur somewhere any day. Congress's ponderousness is so exasperating and inadequate to the times that it is not hard to imagine a throng of young people descending on Washington and, rather than marching in the streets, quietly but firmly pushing into the two legislative

Government: Rebuilding the One-Hoss Shay

chambers and staging a sit-down to dramatize the nation's impatience.

A third major area of inadequacy is the bureaucracy: the executive departments and the federal agencies. Their mandates and scope of action have little relationship to the great gamut of environmental problems. They are fraught with paralyzing conflicts of interest. Some of the principal departments—for instance, Agriculture, Interior, and Commerce—were set up to foster commercial interests. Over the years they have become the creatures of these interests. They are still preoccupied with promotion even though the environmental crisis has shifted the weight of need to regulation.

Pesticide problems stayed on dead center for nearly a decade because such regulatory authority as there was was centered in the Department of Agriculture, handmaiden of pesticide users.

The creation of the independent Environmental Protection Agency late in 1970 was an initial step toward reconciling such conflicts. But it was far from a comprehensive step. The EPA was given jurisdiction over air pollution, water pollution, solid waste, pesticides, radiation, and noise. But this did nothing about nonpollutional aspects of environment, such as resources and land use. And it fell far short of dispelling bureaucratic schizophrenia.

The Department of the Interior still has the dual, contradictory responsibilities of conserving much of the public domain while functioning as the servant of interests like the mining industry, which has a capacious record of despoiling the public domain.

The U.S. Forest Service, within the Department of Agriculture, still has the contradictory functions of preserving the national forests and assisting the timber industry in wholesale tree-cutting.

This built-in bias toward commercial interests is reinforced by a host of industry advisory boards with quasi-official roles in policy formation among federal agencies. These panels' deliberations and exertions of pressure on the agencies are often deliberately obscured from the public view.

In concept these panels are as fallacious as the "stacked" state pollution boards; the only basic difference is that the federal advisory bodies do not have statutory authority. They are premised on the theory of providing expertise (which the governmental agencies might get better elsewhere) and on the notion that special economic interests need governmental assistance and deserve special representation. In the context of today, when all our basic industries have demonstrated their ability to survive and flourish, their special entree, as opposed to consideration of the general welfare, is a negation of our other tenets of representative government.

If commercial interests' proposals cannot prevail in the regular legislative forums (where these interests already have exceptional entree and influence), either they deserve to be rejected or the legislative processes need to be changed. The philosophy of special privilege should be resoundingly repudiated, and the clamor and pressures of the Environmental Revolution will not modulate until this comes about.

All the nominal environmental reforms so far have done little toward curbing the natural instincts of the federal bureaucracy toward self-aggrandizement.

Agencies like the Army Corps of Engineers and the Bureau of Reclamation (in Interior) exist essentially by concocting projects with which to occupy themselves. The Corps

Government: Rebuilding the One-Hoss Shay

of Engineers, in its domestic civilian functions, is one of the largest lower-echelon spending agencies, disbursing over $1 billion a year. And it is one of the most anomalous. It consists of a couple of hundred officers, who in laughable theory are getting military experience, and 40,000 civilian employees, whose chief function is planning earth-moving projects and parceling out contracts to private firms to execute them.

While some of this work is useful, the Corps's outlandish forays have been many and classic. It proposed the building of no fewer than four hundred dams along the four hundred-mile length of the Potomac River. It campaigned for years for an immense dam that would have turned a large portion of Alaska into a lake. For more than a generation—until President Nixon halted construction in 1971—the Corps pursued a project to build a canal across the head of the Florida peninsula from the Atlantic to the Gulf of Mexico. It continued spending millions on the project and inflicting great environmental damage in the face of mountains of testimony over the years from independent experts that the project was useless.

Ever since the Hoover Commission days of the 1930's there have been proposals to get the Engineers out of civilian activities and assign the work more logically. But the Corps, through its historic venal reciprocal-back-scratching ties with members of Congress, has hung on.

The environmental outrages of these various agencies were moderated by the establishment of the Council on Environmental Quality, with the requirement that federal agencies submit environmental-impact prospectuses on their projects. But these declarations are not conclusive. The Council is adviser to the President, and he can ignore its judgments. And however effectively the Council functions, the fact remains that some of the projects that come before it should not even be initiated.

Even within the executive departments' proper spheres of operation there is an appalling tradition of tacit bureaucratic arrogance. An example was the recent evolution of the Mineral King resort plan in the Sequoia national forest in California. The Forest Service, which had sponsored the development by private concessionaires of eighty ski resorts in national forests, came up with plans for a $3-million development in Mineral King Valley, a remote, narrow canyon in the Sierra Nevada.

No public hearings were held on whether the development was advisable. But under the usual procedures a concessionaire—the Walt Disney organization—was selected to build it. Thereupon the bureaucratic iron curtain descended on all the planning for three years. When the curtain rose in 1969 it transpired that in backstage negotiations the Disney people had persuaded the Forest Service to enlarge the original $3 million concept to a $30 million project, with a capacity of a million visitors a year.

There has been heated debate between some conservation groups and the federal government over whether Mineral King should be changed from a wilderness area to a tourist attraction at all. But the main point is that the valley's size is immutable, and that an area that might readily accommodate a $3 million development wouldn't necessarily accommodate one ten times as big. Yet the decision to pursue the bigger plan was no more open to public opinion than it would have been in the Soviet Union.

President Nixon in 1971 proposed a sweeping reorganiza-

Government: Rebuilding the One-Hoss Shay

tion of the Executive Branch of the federal government into four basic divisions, one of which would handle natural resources. The proposals were based on a thorough study by an advisory panel of business experts. Its chairman, Roy Ash, commented: "Departments originally created to emphasize the distinctions between urban and rural interests, industry and agriculture, small business and large business, management and labor, no longer reflect the kinds of conflict that must rise to the presidential level in all their details. . . ."

The structure of the executive departments, he added, "should be clearly geared to the major and central purposes of government today rather than guided by historical or subordinate purposes, by narrow constituencies, or by letting themselves become a purpose (bureaucracy in its least responsive sense)."

Some of the more enlightened members of Congress also were demanding reforms in its out-dated processes. Here again the big issue was relinquishments of areas of sovereignty by their traditional possessors.

One big question was whether this could be accomplished at all. The other question was whether it could be accomplished in time to meet the inexorable demands of the environmental crisis and the Environmental Revolution.

13

International Action: The Coming Showdown

THE PRINCIPAL environmental problems transcend national boundaries in several ways.

Air and water recognize no governmental lines. Effluvia from German industry recurrently afflict a half-dozen neighboring countries. The DDT found in Antarctica may have come from farms in the United States or malaria-ridden swamps in Asia.

There are contaminants that linger in the atmosphere indefinitely, moving around the globe from their points of origin. If the atmosphere becomes too contaminated, it could alter global climate patterns. Scientists are not sure which effect might prevail, but the dirty air could keep out solar heat and might cause a general cooling, or it could trap heat (the "greenhouse effect") that the earth normally radiates to maintain the temperature range that sustains human life.

The relatively thin envelope of air that surrounds the earth is one common global resource, like a gold mine worked by

International Action: The Coming Showdown

everyone and from which no person can rightly be excluded, because its product is so vital. Similarly the oceans are a reservoir of common resources—fish, mammals, reptiles, vegetation, and minerals.

The last million years or so have really been a "grace period" in which humanity was small enough so that there were plenty of these resources for everybody.

Now there aren't. Many people are contaminating air and water that other people have an inherent human right to receive in a pure state. Some of these common resources are being exploited and plundered by a minority of unscrupulous entrepreneurs. The near-extinction of some kinds of whales, the decimation of the Atlantic salmon, and inroads on seals and sea otters are examples.

In effect, anarchy has prevailed in respect to these resources. International regulation of their use plainly is vital.

There are other levels at which international collaboration is in order. Man's knowledge of how to deal with environmental problems is in many respects scanty. They can be jointly explored, with saving of time and money to everyone, and the findings shared.

Also the world's nations have many superficially internal environmental problems that can be advantageously dealt with cooperatively: conserving the productivity of soils, conserving animals, conserving geological wonders and scientific and historic sites that are a legitimate interest of the world community.

In 1963 President John F. Kennedy, in an unusual presidential appearance before the United Nations General Assembly, urged international action to preserve the human environment.

This was nine weeks before he was assassinated. Under the

ensuing administration his broad-gauged ideas on environmental collaboration were, in the words of one federal official, "quietly shelved" in favor of such specific international gestures as President Johnson's barren global "Water For Peace" program. It was not until 1968, when Sweden proposed a world conference on environmental problems in 1972, that the question of concerted international action was raised before the U.N. again.

In the intervening five years, evidence had piled up rapidly that, to solve the leading environmental problems, action at the national level was not going to be enough. In Europe, aggravated pollution of the Rhine River affected the Netherlands as well as Germany. People in West Germany complained about air pollution wafting down from Holland, and Sweden complained about effluvia from Germany. The Torrey Canyon oil tanker spill afflicted the coasts of both France and England.

In North America the deterioration of the Great Lakes spanned the boundary between the United States and Canada. Scientists found accumulations of DDT in tissues of Antarctic penguins, and in other birds and fish in many places, which could have originated anywhere in the world. The explorer Thor Heyerdahl reported seeing growing patches of chronic pollution on the high seas.

Many international agencies interested themselves in these problems, including numerous affiliates of the United Nations. The North Atlantic Treaty Organization began looking into ocean pollution. The seventeen-nation Council of Europe held a series of conferences on environmental problems, and in July 1970 obtained agreement-in-principle by fifteen nations on a program of stricter controls on the manu-

International Action: The Coming Showdown

facture and sale of pesticides. (The abstaining nations were Switzerland and the Netherlands, both with big chemical industries.)

The twenty-two nation Organization for Economic Cooperation and Development, based in Paris, mounted a two-year scientific study of air pollution problems. Simultaneously the World Meteorological Organization, a United Nations agency based in Geneva, announced a plan for a global network of observation stations in remote areas to produce "baseline" data on the quality of the world's air in its less polluted manifestations. Two months later, the U.N.'s Educational, Scientific and Cultural Organization announced an international study of the Mediterranean Sea, to be supervised by its seventy-nation Oceanographic Commission. Since then there have been countless other multinational projects launched by the seemingly endless profusion of international agencies.

All this was better than nothing. But the most conspicuous feature of all these efforts was their fragmentation, either functional or jurisdictional. Generally they were dealing with problems in terms of narrow specialized missions. A classic example was the case of the U.N.'s Food and Agriculture Organization, which was continuing to espouse the use of DDT at the very time several nations were planning to ban it—simply because the FAO's frame of reference concerned the development of crops, rather than human welfare as a whole.

The need for a better international approach was boldly enunciated by the then United Nations Secretary General, U Thant, in an address at the University of Texas on May 14, 1970. He said:

MADMAN IN A LIFEBOAT

We need a global authority with the support and agreement of governments and of other powerful interests, which can pull together all the piecemeal efforts now being made and which can fill in the gaps where something needs to be done.

This authority must embark expeditiously . . . on the delicate process of reaching a workable compromise among governments and interests on matters affecting the environment. It should be able, if necessary, to police and enforce its decisions. . . .

I believe that a global authority for the protection of the environment should be closely associated with the United Nations [which] for all its shortcomings is the nearest thing we have to a world organization—the only forum where the development of world order is continuously discussed and actively striven for.

Thant, of all people, undoubtedly was aware that anything as definitive as he limned would be a long time materializing. But probably in the spirit of Browning's ". . . a man's reach should exceed his grasp, or what's a heaven for?", he had delineated an inevitable goal.

Just how distant that goal was became evident as the U.N. got down to firm planning for the Stockholm Conference. The task of breathing life and substance into the conference proposal was assigned—at U Thant's suggestion—by the General Assembly in January 1970 to a dynamic and adroit coordinator, Maurice Strong, a dapper, youthful Canadian industrial tycoon-turned-diplomat.

His initial hurdles plainly were, first, to persuade a meaningful proportion of the U.N.'s membership to participate in the conference; and, second, to assure that it would be more than just another of the cliché-ridden talk-fests that international meetings are prone to lapse into when they are confronted with difficult problems.

Two inherent problems of the Stockholm project were the

International Action: The Coming Showdown

cleavage between the Communist and non-Communist blocs, and the even deeper gulf between the handful of "developed," industrialized, relatively affluent nations and the flock of "developing" countries—in plain English the poor, backward have-nots, who constitute upward of 70 per cent of the world's people. The Communists seized upon their very participation at Stockholm (as they habitually seize on everything) as a lever for diplomatic bargaining.

With the have-not nations, there was an even more fundamental basis for wariness: the notion that, in promoting environmental improvement, the rich nations were asking them to indulge in a luxury they could ill afford. In the backward countries, belching smokestacks, however obnoxious, were a welcome symbol of progress, even as in the United States until fairly recent years pollution was depicted as an inevitable concomitant of prosperity.

However firmly entrenched, that feeling was erroneous. What the affluent countries in effect were saying to the backward nations was: "Don't make the same mistakes we did. We've found out the hard way that prosperity is a delusion if it's gained at the cost of a livable environment. We're discovering belatedly that it's a lot less expensive to safeguard environment as you progress than to have to undo your mistakes."

Maurice Strong put together a twenty-seven-nation preparatory committee to map out the agenda of the conference; made sure at the outset that the assemblage would not be sterile by incorporating into the agenda several international compacts on conservation and kindred subjects that had long been under negotiation and were near consummation; and dispelled much of the "emerging" nations' misgivings at a preliminary series of regional symposiums around the world. The committee held four long sessions in the eighteen-month preparatory period.

The Soviet Union and its satellites, while occasionally cantankerous, gave many evidences of feeling they had far more to gain by supporting the Stockholm meeting than by trying to torpedo it.

A big boost for the historic gathering came when, late in 1971, the People's Republic of China, comprising over 20 per cent of the world's people, was admitted to the U.N., rounding out the prospective participation at Stockholm to include almost all the nations of the world. The speeches, discussions, and debates during the preparatory sessions, however, underscored the fact that the nations were not ready to underwrite any such global environmental authority as U Thant had outlined, however inevitable it might ultimately be. The predominant theme at these meetings was that a majority of nations were all for various degrees of collaboration, but were opposed to the slightest relinquishment of national sovereignty.

Anticipating this, Maurice Strong disclaimed any aims of setting up any sort of environmental "superagency" within the U.N., even for collaborative purposes. The goal he stressed was for agreement on various objectives in terms of environmental security, and on various degrees of action toward them; with at most, in the way of superstructure, a smallish coordinating unit in the U.N., and with concerted international action to be arrived at through existing U.N. procedures.

Twelve hundred representatives of 113 nations met for two weeks in Stockholm in June, 1972, and in what many observ-

International Action: The Coming Showdown

ers considered an epochal parley reached virtually unanimous agreement on all the major items that Strong had blueprinted: a "Declaration of Principles" of international environmental responsibility; a program of over 100 specific proposals for international action to improve and protect the environment; and organizational details of a new U.N. unit to coordinate these activities and develop new programs.

Beyond Stockholm, what is the outlook for truly global collaboration and coordination?

Soothsayers disagree.

"What is needed," James Reston wrote late in 1970, "is a broad general agreement between Washington and Moscow to get the threats of war, hunger and overpopulation under control. But this is not in the cards for the foreseeable future."

But a luminary in the field of international finance, A. W. Clausen, president of the huge Bank of America, foresaw environment leading politics.

The planet's ecology is unimpressed by political boundaries and subdivisions [he told an international banking meeting in Tokyo]. A multi-national challenge dictates a multi-national response. And this necessity in itself will shape the economic and political accommodations we will be making over the remainder of this century.

The international aspects of environmental problems is such that I can even envisage the desirability of creating a supra-national entity similar to the International Monetary Fund to assume prompt cooperative action in this field.

There is a possibility that the world is resolving the environmental predicament, almost in spite of itself, by a subtle process of boring from within. We may find some day that

MADMAN IN A LIFEBOAT

our multitude of fragmented approaches has left us with only the problem of formal coordination of them.

But this seems a slender hope to cling to.

In the United States we frequently tax ourselves with being a "crisis-oriented" society that reacts chiefly to emergencies. But this is less an American trait than a human one. No nation has a historic reputation for foresight. It may take an international environmental catastrophe to precipitate effective international action and real collaboration. The prayer is that it would not be too big a one.

Nature has no tolerance for madmen in lifeboats.

14

Citizen Action: The Key to Tomorrow

> *"You pay your taxes and you hope your government will look out for your interests. But now we find we have to give our time, money and effort to fight the things the government is supposed to be protecting us from."* A Los Angeles housewife involved in a conservation controversy.

THE BIGGEST misconception that is delaying thoroughgoing environmental reform is the notion that government, on its own initiative, will take care of the whole thing. The fact is that government, left to its own devices, allowed the nation to drift into the present environmental predicament.

There are some valid technical reasons for this apparent dereliction.

Government's primary function is not to be creative but to reconcile conflicting interests. And there are just as many interests in our society today that would degrade the environment—always in the exalted name of "progress"—as there are interests that would improve it.

There is industry. There is agriculture, with its pesticides, its seasonal field-burning, its uncontrolled animal wastes. There are the highway and canal builders. And a host of others.

Up to now, the destructive interests have held sway in the halls of government. ("The corporation's convenience has been allowed to rule national policy," wrote the President's Science Advisory Committee in its 1965 report, "Restoring the Quality of Our Environment.") Except for a few conservation organizations whose voice historically has been weak, those who would protect and improve the quality of life have let the battle go by default.

The process by which this happens is very simple. Every session of Congress or the average state legislature considers several thousand bills. The average legislator has time to make a personal study of the merits of only a handful of these measures. For the rest, he is dependent on what people tell him. There are trickles of information from citizen constituents. But the people who are closest to him, day in and day out, year in and year out, are the lobbyists and other representatives of organized "interests." Thus it is quite possible that on a given issue, unless it is a *cause célèbre,* a legislator will hear only one side of the story. And that is the way he is likely, in the best of conscience, to vote.

Of course horse-trading among legislators is part of the regular pattern. And many legislators are biased from the outset toward interests that help elect them. But on a given issue, considering a legislative body as a whole, such influences tend to cancel each other out, and a reasonable proposal starts with a fifty-fifty chance.

Only when aroused public opinion expresses itself clearly and emphatically will the scales necessarily end up swinging

Citizen Action: The Key to Tomorrow

the right way. Accordingly, the vital ingredient in the Environmental Revolution, if it is to produce constructive results, is citizen action.

The citizen who wants to advance the cause of environmental quality does not have to wait for action from Washington or the state capital. Environmental quality begins at home. Many who lament the state of our environment, and government's slowness in doing anything about it, don't even know the names of their congressmen or state legislators.

Even fewer, perhaps, know where their local sewage plant is and what sort of treatment it is giving sewage; or just where their local drinking water supply comes from and what kind of treatment it gets. And how many know anything about the finances of their municipal trash removal system?

Concerned citizens, at the cost of no more than a little time, could familiarize themselves with these facts. Because this is where much of the nation's environmental degradation starts.

They also would do well to familiarize themselves with local and state air and water pollution laws, as to their content and their enforcement. Under existing laws, virtually all definitive state and local governmental actions on air and water pollution can be taken only after public hearings. Citizens who ignore these hearings are not in a position to criticize the results.

Every citizen can't attend every hearing. But it's not difficult for citizens to band together to share the work and make sure that no hearing goes unmonitored and no opportunity is missed to present points of view.

Through such activities, local and regional sources of air and water pollution can be pinpointed and it can be determined whether these sources are in compliance with existing laws or are operating under "variances" (temporary permits to violate the law) and are maintaining promised clean-up schedules.

Pollution is not the only area that can be covered by such activity. The same governmental processes apply to zoning, highway building, and other aspects of environmental management.

So much for the local level.

When it comes to state and federal activity the individual citizen tends to feel helpless. "What can one person do?" is the perpetual question.

A realistic answer is that, in influencing state and federal legislation, one lone citizen cannot do much. But we have 200 million "lone citizens" in this country. A senator has on average two million constituents. A representative has about 400,000 constituents. In California, the most populous state, a state senator has 500,000 constituents, a state assemblyman 250,000. If legislators and administrators listened to all of these "lone" constituents they would have time for nothing else and the cacophony would be deafening.

That, to a considerable degree, is what has been happening on a national scale in connection with environmental problems. So it is hardly surprising that results have been indifferent.

There is a very simple solution to this problem. That is for citizens to *organize:* to join existing organizations concerned about the environment, such as the Sierra Club, the National Audubon Society, the Izaak Walton League, the League of Women Voters. Or, alternatively, citizens can form their own ad hoc organizations to push particular causes. Legislators listen to organizations and groups. They represent blocs of votes. And because they are organized, they may be a

Citizen Action: The Key to Tomorrow

better source of the information and sentiment legislators are usually seeking than the lone man-in-the-street.

Listening doesn't necessarily mean accepting a group's arguments. That is dependent on three factors:

- How substantial the organization is in terms of membership;
- How well the members have done their homework on the issues they are dealing with;
- How much contact such groups maintain with key legislators.

An occasional letter, even from a large group, isn't enough. There has to be regular personal contact with legislators, to match the personal contacts regularly maintained by the "interests." This isn't difficult. In Washington this is best done through existing organizations, most of which have regular liaison with Capitol Hill.

In state capitals, a sizable citizen group can hire its own lobbyist. Most lobbyists represent a number of clients, so the cost is much less than a full salary. If a group can't afford a lobbyist, its members at least can maintain contact through legislators' field offices, and by delegating emissaries to the state capital, to talk with legislators and especially to monitor legislative proceedings.

"Legislators invariably conduct their business a lot differently," one of them remarked candidly, "when they know they're being watched."

Many citizens naïvely place their reliance entirely on testimony at legislative hearings. Veteran legislators will tell you that this is a mistake. Testimony should be presented if only for the publicity it gets with the public. But most legislators will have swung to a point of view before a hearing takes place. Witnesses then are fighting an uphill battle to change these preconceived opinions. That is why day-in day-out contact, between hearings, is important.

The record is full of dramatic examples of what such citizen pressures can do.

In San Francisco not long ago a few hundred citizens banded together to fight interests that were ruining San Francisco Bay with landfills and pollution. The group conducted a good publicity campaign to rally public support. More importantly, the group kept bird-dogging developments at the state capital, where several bills had been introduced to "Save the Bay."

The adversaries, who included some of the nation's largest corporate interests and some of California's biggest municipalities, mounted the most elaborate lobbying operation they could. The citizens had only the part-time services of one lobbyist. But by backing him up with sedulous citizen action, they beat the "interest lobby" and got a law passed creating a supervisory agency to "Save the Bay."

The same strategy will work on a smaller scale. In Los Angeles a group of about two hundred boat and home owners—headed by only a dozen or so real activists—who for years had been showered with sulfuric acid from the smokestacks of a power plant, forced one of the nation's biggest electric companies to switch to clean fuel. They did it simply by attending, for the first time, the public hearings where the power company for years had been automatically getting variance permits to burn dirty fuel. The citizens simply asked "Why?" and proved that this was unnecessary.

In Washington, ad hoc coalitions of citizens and conservation organizations succeeded in pushing a water pollution

Citizen Action: The Key to Tomorrow

appropriation up from the meager $250 million President Nixon had asked for to $800 million.

They threw road blocks in the way of the supersonic transport project. And they twice repelled a timber industry bill —presold even to the White House and the Department of Agriculture—which they considered a raid on the national forests.

It can be done. The big problem is that up to the last few years the public as a whole has neglected to use this elementary tool of the democratic process, even while lamenting that it was being excluded from "decision-making."

Finally, citizens have the avenue of legal action.

In the last few years suits by citizens, often in collaboration with conservation organizations, have stopped the construction of highways, canals, islands, and commercial developments on public lands, and also have brought many polluters to book.

Environmental law is still in the process of development and definition. But the same basic principles apply to it as apply to all law. Its purpose is to compel the application of existing statutes, to prevent foreseeable injuries, and to provide compensation for injuries that have occurred.

But environmental problems have been forcing conceptual changes in the law. Air pollution, for instance, once was simply a question of individual (or corporation) A emitting fumes that bothered individual B. B traditionally had to prove tangible damage—that the fumes had affected his health, peeled paint off his house, or damaged his crops. Sometimes even this wasn't enough. In the case of crop damage, for instance, a court might hold that A's economic interests were more important from a public standpoint than B's crops.

Several new elements have entered the picture. One is that the victim of a polluter's fumes need not be just another individual, whose interests can be weighed against the polluter's, but a whole community.

Second, the concept that the damage must be measurable in economic terms has become obsolete: imponderable esthetic values, such as destruction of a beautiful view or a recreational area, are acknowledged to be important.

Third, the concept is gaining acceptance that the public has an inalienable right to an environment unsullied by individuals' self-serving activities.

Finally, only a party showing a substantial personal interest in a situation could come into court to complain about it. Now third parties, such as conservation organizations, can take up the cudgels on behalf of the general public. In the Mineral King case in California the Sierra Club challenged the legality of a resort development in a national forest, acting on behalf of the general public, who were the real owners of the forest.

Several states have taken steps to clarify the legal ground rules on environmental situations, either by adopting laws expressly permitting citizens to sue (in state courts), or by adopting constitutional provisions covering citizens' rights to a pleasant environment, which can provide a basis for legal actions. Similar measures are pending in several states, and in Congress in relation to the federal courts.

Even in the present gray state of the law, it can be said broadly that when what some people consider an environmental outrage is being committed, some legal grounds for suit usually can be found.

Meanwhile, in connection particularly with water pollution, citizens have express sanction to sue under the Refuse

Citizen Action: The Key to Tomorrow

section of the 1899 Act, which forbids the discharge of fluid wastes except municipal sewage into waterways without a federal permit. The law says that a citizen with evidence of an objectionable discharge not covered by a permit can take that evidence (customarily in affidavit form) to the local United States District Attorney. If the latter does not act against the alleged violator within a reasonable time, the citizen can bring his own suit against the offender and if he wins can collect half the statutory fine, which goes up to $2,500 for each day's violation. This kind of action is called a "qui tam" suit, meaning "he who sues in the name of the government."

Some people have suggested that such "informer" suits are immoral. But the concept of the "qui tam" action is hallowed in law, going back to ancient England, as a means by which citizens can assist the government.

Under the 1899 Act, the Hudson River Fisherman's Association in New York collected $2,000 as its share of a fine imposed on the Penn Central Railroad for polluting the Hudson River. Many other such suits are pending.

William D. Ruckelshaus of the EPA has said, "I am heartily in favor of responsible citizen court action against polluters—of citizen action against government at every level, including the Federal government and my own agency."

Citizen action is not only appropriate but vital. Environmental problems are so extensive that government is now the medium through which remedial efforts must be coordinated. And government in a democracy is entirely an instrument of its citizens. It is what they make it.

Russell Train, chairman of the Council on Environmental Quality, said in 1971:

MADMAN IN A LIFEBOAT

The cause of environment is one which the citizens have made. No political leader, no government official, can take sole credit for putting the environment on the national agenda.

Citizens identified problems, organized to influence governmental actions, made themselves heard at public hearings, brought actions before administrative agencies and in the courts, and helped the press to interpret their concerns.

The measure of citizens' strength today is the government's respect for them. It is simply inconceivable that any agency of government or elected official could turn back the clock and ignore the environmental concerns of citizens for very long. The courts, the press, and the people simply wouldn't allow it.

An informed, concerned and responsible citizenry is the crucial factor upon which ultimately all environmental progress must depend.

Some Sources

(The sources of many of the references in this book either are evident or are readily available through such standard works as Presidential Documents and the New York Times Index. Following are some helpful specific sources.)

Council on Environmental Quality. Annual reports, 1970 et seq.

Ehrlich, Paul. *Population/Resources/Environment.* San Francisco, W.H. Freeman, 1970.

Federal Water Quality Administration (now Environmental Protection Agency). "Feasibility of Alternative Means of Cooling for Thermal Power Plants Near Lake Michigan." Report. August, 1970.

Hill, Gladwin. *Our Troubled Waters.* Public Affairs Committee (New York) Pamphlet 462. 1971.

Laycock, George. *The Diligent Destroyers.* New York, Doubleday, 1970.

Marine, Gene. *America the Raped.* New York, Avon, 1970.

National Academy of Sciences. *Resources and Man.* W.H. Freeman, 1970.

———. *Waste Management and Control.* National Academy, 1966.

O'Connor, John, and Cinatrella, Joseph (of the National Air Pollution Control Administration—now Environmental Protection Agency). "An Air Pollution Control Cost Study." *Journal of the Air Pollution Control Association,* May, 1970.

Solid Waste Management, U.S. Bureau of (now Environmental Protection Agency). "The Role of Packaging in Solid Waste Management," 1966 to 1976. Report. 1969.

Wager, J. Alan. "Growth versus the Quality of Life." *Science Magazine,* June 5, 1970.

Index

"Activated sludge" process, 50
Agriculture, and water pollution, 51–52
Air pollution, 41–47, 109; and air standards, 73; clean-up cost, 63, 64–65, 66; control act, 45; densities, 43; legislation, 88
Alabama, 74–75, 76–77
Alaska, 73
Aluminum Company of America, 75, 77
Anaconda Company, 74–75
Army Corps of Engineers, 10, 54, 90–91
Arizona, 73
Ash, Roy, 93
Automobile industry, and smog, 44–46

Berry, Phillip, 85
Bethlehem Steel, 74
"Biological oxygen demand" (BOD), 52
Borlaug, Dr. Norman, 16
Bottles, nonreturnable, 9
Bowaters Southern Paper Corporation, 77
Bureau of Reclamation, 90
Bureaucracy, problem of government, 89–90

Cain, Stanley, 14
Capitalism, and pollution, 80–85
Castle Peak (Idaho), 27
Chicago, and land use authority, 33
Citizen action, 11, 103–12
City, development of new, 36–37
Clausen, A. W., 101
Cloud, Dr. Preston, 25
Colorado River Commission, 48
Commoner, Dr. Barry, 53
Communists, and Stockholm Conference, 99

Congress, 87 ff. *See also* Federal government
Connecticut, 76
"Conservation vote," 11
Council of Europe, 96

DDT, 96, 97
Denver, 57
Detergents, phosphate, 9
Dominick, David, 75
Donora, Pa., air pollution incident in, 41, 44
Dumping, solid waste, 57 *See also* Rail haul plans
Du Pont, 77

Earth Day, 8
Economy, and effects of pollution control costs on, 66 ff.
Educational, Scientific and Cultural Organization, 97
Ehrlich, Dr. Paul, 14–16
England, 96
Environmental crisis, 3–6, 7–12
Environmental degradation, 9–10
Environmental law, citizen's recourse to, 109–11
Environmental policies, 11
Environmental Protection Agency, 9, 53, 59, 76, 89
Environmental reform, 11 12; cost of, 63 ff.; implementation of, 70–78
Environmental Revolution, 7, 11, 21, 79, 81, 82, 84, 86, 90

Fallout pollution, 52
"Family planning," 20
Federal government: implementation of environmental reform, 70–78; and

115

INDEX

Federal *cont'd*
  land-use management, 32 ff.; vs. states, 82
Federal program for waste management, 61–62
Federal Water pollution abatement hearings, 71, 72
Federal Water Quality Administration, 53
Florida, 73
Food: production, 15–16; supply, diminishing, 14
Food and Agricultural Organization, 97
Fortune, 21
France, 96
Free enterprise, and pollution, 80–85
Free market price system, 25–26

Gasoline engine, and air pollution, 46
General Motors, 80
Gilbertson, Wesley, 59
Government action, 9–10, 86–93; and citizen action, 103 ff.; and water pollution, 54–55 *See also* Federal government, State government
Grain, 15
Great Lakes, 96
Green Revolution, 16

Haagen-Smit, Dr. Arie, 44–45
Hanks, James, 63–64
Harvard Business Review, 63
Hawaii, 73
Heyerdahl, Thor, 96
Hickel, J. Walter, 54
"High air pollution potential" (HAAP), 43
Holland, 96
Homestead Act, 32
Hoover Commission, 91
Housing Act of 1970, 38
Hudson River Fisherman's Association, 111
"Hydrologic cycle," 49

Illinois, 73, 77
Industrial Revolution, 8
Industry, 11, 26, 79–85; advisory boards, 90; control of state regulatory

Industry *cont'd*
  boards, 73–77; cost of pollution clean-up, 64–65; and water pollution, 49–55 *See also* Automobile industry, Oil industry
"Informer" suits, 111
International assistance programs, 14
International regulation, 94–102
Inventory, land, 32–34
Izaak Walton League, 106

Jackson, Henry, 39
Johnson, C. C., Jr., 38–39
Johnson, Lyndon B., 96

Kansas, 73
Kennedy, John F., 95
Kentucky, 74
Kube, Harold, 63–64

Labor, 11
Lake Superior, pollution of, 27
Lake Tahoe, 50
Land, use of, 30–40
Land-use management, 33 ff.
Las Vegas Wash, 49–50
Laws, problems of implementing, 70 ff.
League of Women Voters, 106
Legislation, 88; citizen's influence on, 104–5
London, and air pollution, 41
Los Angeles, 44, 61; citizen action in, 108

Manhattan (N.Y.C.), population density, 31
Maryland, 73
Massachusetts, 73
McCloskey, Michael, 40
Meuse Valley, Belgium, air pollution incident in, 41
Middleton, Dr. John, 75–76
Miller, Leonard, A., 3
Milwaukee, 57
Mineral King resort plan, 92, 110
Monsanto, 77
Montana, 74, 76
Muir, John, 9
Municipal pollution, 52, 53, 54

Index

National Academy of Sciences, 17
National Air Pollution Control Administration, 75
National Audubon Society, 106
National Commission on Urban Growth, 36
National forests, 34
National parks, 34–35
National preserves, 34–35
National priorities, 86–87
National shorelines, 34
National Steel, 74
National Weather Service, 43
Natural pollution, 52
Nevada Power Company, 48–49
New Jersey, 73, 77
New Mexico, 73
Newton, Sir Isaac, 8
New York, 73; air pollution, 41, 43; and dumping space, 57
New York *Times,* 73, 76
Nitrates, 51
Nixon, Richard, 15, 17, 88, 91, 92–93; and land-use problem, 36–39; and water pollution, 55, 87, 109
North Atlantic Treaty Organization (NATO), 96

Oceans: as food source, 16; pollution of, 96
Oil industry, 21–29
Oppenheimer, Jack C., 3
Organization of American States, 15
Organization for Economic Cooperation and Development, 97
Oxides of nitrogen, 67

Packaging, 60
Penn Central, 111
People's Republic of China, 100
Pesticide problems, 89
Philadelphia, 57
Phosphates, 51
Pollution control, 11; cost of, 63–69 *See also* Air Pollution, Solid waste, Water pollution
Population, 5, 11, 13–20; control, 15, 18–19; density, 13, 31; dispersing, 38; projections, 37; rate of increase, 13–14

Population / Resources / Environment (Ehrlich), 15
Potomac River, 87
President's Council on Environmental Quality, 9, 29, 52, 53, 64, 65–66, 69, 91–92, 111
President's Science Advisory Committee, 104
Public awareness, 12
Public hearings, 105
Public land, 34–35
Public Land Law Review Commission, 27, 34–35

"Quality of life," 8
"Qui tam" suit, 111
Quota system, and oil industry, 22 ff.

Rail haul plans, 57
Recycling, 28, 60–61
Resources, exploitation of natural, 21–29
"Resource commission" studies, 28
"Resources and Man" study, 25
Reston, James, 40, 101
"Restoring the Quality of Our Environment" report, 104
Reynolds Metals, 75
Rhine River, 96
Rhode Island, 73
River and Harbor Act of 1899, 10, 54, 110–11
Rubbish, problem of collecting, 56 ff.
Ruckelshaus, William, 76–78, 111

Salt, as contaminant, 51
Santa Barbara, oil drilling off, 21–22, 24
San Bernardino Valley, and air pollution, 42
San Francisco: citizen action in, 108; dumping space, 57
Santee, Calif., 50
Science, 28
Sewage: facilities, 11; treatment, 50–51, 53
Sierra Club, 40, 85, 106, 110
Smog, 42–43, 44–45
Solid waste, 56–62; cost of disposal, 58, 63, 65, 66; load, analysis of, 59
Soot, control, cost of, 67–68

INDEX

Southern California Edison Company, 67
Soviet Union, 80, 100
Stans, Maurice, 28
Starvation, 14
State governments: and implementation of environmental reforms, 70–78; and land-use management, 32 ff.; vs. federal government, 82
State regulation boards, industry's control of, 73–77
Stockholm Conference, 98–101
Strip mining, 27
Strong, Maurice, 98–101
Sulphur dioxides, 67
Sweden, 96

Tennessee, 77
Tertiary sewage treatment, 51
Thant, U, 97–98
Thermal pollution, 67
Train, Russell, 111

Underdeveloped countries, population in, 14
United Nations, 16–17, 95; and international control, 96 ff.
United States, 5; land-use in, 30 ff.; optimum population level, 19, 20
U.S. Agency for International Development, 15
U.S. Department of Agriculture, 89
U.S. Forest Service, 89, 92
U.S. Department of Health, Education and Welfare, 59
U.S. Department of the Interior, 54, 89; Bureau of Land Management, 34–35
U.S. News and World Report, 37
U.S. Steel, 74
Universal Declaration of Human Rights, 17
Urban problems, 5; growth, 36–38; population in, 19, 31 ff.
Utah, 74

Vermont, 73
Virginia, 73

Wagar, J. Alan, 28–29
Walt Disney organization, 92
Washington, 73; citizen action in, 108–9
Waste management program, 61–62
"Water for Peace" program, 96
Water pollution, 42, 48–55, 108–9, 110–11; cost of control, 64–65, 66; legislation, 54–55, 88
Water Quality Act of 1970, 88
Weather, effect of, on air pollution, 42 ff.
West Germany, 96
World conference on environmental problems, 96 ff.
World Meteorological Organization, 97